D1520374

How to Start
an Audiovisual Collection

edited by

MYRA NADLER

The Scarecrow Press, Inc.
Metuchen, N.J. & London
1978

Library of Congress Cataloging in Publication Data

Main entry under title:

How to start an audiovisual collection.

Includes index.
1. Audio-visual library service. 2. Libraries--
Special collections--Non-book materials.
I. Nadler, Myra, 1945-
Z717.H68   025.17'7   78-1993
ISBN 0-8108-1124-3

CONTENTS

iii

PREFACE

An entirely happy enterprise, this book represents the outpourings of a braintrust of bright, imaginative and experienced people whose dedication and joy has been to serve as audiovisual specialists in the library profession. Their names appear elsewhere in this work. To them go applause and warm thanks for their contributions.

With an underlined earnestness, my thanks go also to the Administration and Board of the Palos Verdes Library District, whose willingness to lead and experiment has resulted in a public library that can stand as a model of audiovisual service, a public library where the use of audiovisual materials is as high as that of books in many other comparable libraries.

And affectionate thanks go to Eric and Ilse Moon, the aura of whose friendship and encouragement aided the concept and development of this book.

MN

v

INTRODUCTION

In 1970 I was asked to take over a fledgling audio-visual department in a medium-sized suburban public library. My experience with audiovisual was nil, my fear of equipment and machinery considerable. I gained courage and knowledge from visiting public school, academic and special library media departments, talking to audiovisual librarians and reading everything on the subject. Since then, I, along with many other non-audiovisual librarians, have come a long way toward understanding the functions, appeal and need for media in library collections. Some material is only available on tape or film. Some people can look or listen, but cannot or will not read.

This book is intended to help anyone needing to start or implement audiovisual collections or services. It is for the librarian or administrator inexperienced in the audio-visual arena. It is not theoretical; rather it is a how-to manual, written by people who have done it and are still at it. It tells how to establish basic collections, which indexes and review media to use. It tells what equipment you'll need and which specific makes and models to buy--and why. It tells how to staff departments, plan services, organize programs--and how to publicize it all. The information is practical and current; the emphasis is pragmatic.

Myra Nadler

Chapter 1

THE BASIC AUDIOVISUAL MATERIALS COLLECTION:
SELECTION, EVALUATION, ORGANIZATION

Helen W. Cyr

As in other sections of this book the underlying prem-
ise in these pages is that the public library audiovisual materials collection should be handled on an equal footing with
the library's print materials. That means that planning,
budgeting, and staff interest and knowledge of audiovisual
materials ought to be comparable in scope and quality with
similar efforts directed to books, pamphlets, and serials.
Accordingly, the suggestions for audiovisual collection building made here reflect the care and concern for judgment
that we hope are expended on the library's other media.
The audiovisual collection is not a frivolous frill added as a
decorator adds "accent" to a room but a significant partner
in the business of supplying information and recreation to
the public. At least fifteen percent of the library's resources
budget should be reserved for audiovisual materials. [1]

Selection Policy

Before starting to build the audiovisual materials collection the library staff should think through a course of action that outlines the institution's philosophy of AV services
in terms of the community to be served, the goals and capa-

bilities of the library developing the plan, and the characteristics and potential use of various audiovisual formats:
films, recordings, videotapes, and the like. It is senseless
to buy items that will not be used because they do not match
the interests of the public to be served or because they cannot be played or projected outside the library premises due
to lack of available equipment in the community.

Indeed, knowledge of the local region and its inhabit-
ants is particularly important for planning the AV collection
since AV materials are on the average more expensive per
unit than print materials and the need to avoid poor buys is
consequently greater. The library staff will find the socio-
economic range and proportions of population of each stratum
are indicators of accompanying informational needs and social problems. The community's employment profile not only
tells how the people earn their living but suggests aspirations
and interests.

What is the age range of the community? Is it loaded
with senior citizens? Or the reverse--full of young couples
with children? Typical experience of libraries, supported by
statistical evidence, shows that the audiovisual materials requirements for children--both those materials used directly
by them and items used by adults for juvenile audiences--far
exceed those for any other age group (over twenty-five per
cent of total 16mm film use in some libraries, for example).
What is the ethnic make-up of the area's public? Obviously
a good materials collection must be broad enough to satisfy
general needs, but also specific enough to take care of significant numbers of special groups, such as Polish Ameri-
cans, blacks, Spanish-speaking peoples, and others.

What are the recreational and cultural offerings in
the area? Are there theaters, cultural societies, clubs,

museums, galleries within easy driving distance? What are
the entertainment preferences? If the library is located in
a cultural "wasteland," the course of action will be considerably different from that for a library community bustling with
artistic activity. The lack of a movie theater within a radius
of fifty miles would indicate that the library has an important
role to play in obtaining 16mm feature-length, theatrical
films, both old and current productions. On the other hand,
in a town or region with several movie theaters and an active
film society the library will probably limit acquisitions of
theatrical films to older classics that pose no threat of competition to local theater owners and, instead, concentrate on
informational (nonfiction) or short fictional movies.

The AV facilities of local educational institutions--
public, private, colleges, universities--should be examined.
Do they have audiotapes, videotapes, 16mm films? Does
every school have a media center? If not, what is the source
of audiovisual material for the schools? Will they want to
borrow what you have? Will you want to lend materials to
them? Some libraries do, some don't. Such matters must
be decided, for subject matter and emphasis will be influenced by these factors. A very small library system might
choose to create a cooperative service with local schools
and colleges, for example. The public library is encouraged
not to assume responsibility for school curriculum materials
provision unless such a cooperative arrangement is made.

Once the audiovisual collection is developed the library
will find that clubs, civic organizations, hospitals, and
churches, if any, are active borrowers. It makes good sense,
therefore, to be aware in advance of demand of the existence
of groups and agencies so that appropriate materials will be
on hand.

Local availability of AV equipment, such as video cassette playback units, can determine what the library's role in
regard to video software will be.   The Public Library Association's published standards[2] make specific quantitative recommendations.   However, lack of playback facilities outside the
library indicates that the video cassette collection may have
to be used exclusively on the library premises and that the
materials selected will have to be appealing enough to attract
patrons despite limiting factors.   Perhaps the library staff
will find the effort to sustain this service too great and will
want to delay video software acquisitions until general conditions can be improved.   Planning should, above all, be
realistic.   Rather than spread itself too thin and accomplish
nothing, the library must do everything possible to assure
success of beginning AV collections.

The institution's goals and concept of public service
will also color the audiovisual materials selection policy.
For example, does the staff already endorse the traditional
"balanced" collection as a suitable approach for print materials?   Or is the library attached to the idea of multiple copies
of items in greatest demand as the chief goal in acquisitions?
Will the treatment of AV services be compatible?

Yet another concern is the library's relationship to
its neighbor libraries.   Is it part of a network?   Are there
any film centers in the same region?   Are there implica-
tions for forming a cooperative film service with other agencies?   What are the special features of the other libraries'
audiovisual collections?

Somewhere in the evolution of a materials selection
policy the staff ought to state its position toward the quantitative standards for each audiovisual format as presented in
the Public Library Association's Recommendations for Audio-

visual Materials and Services for Small and Medium-Sized
Public Libraries, [3] the source for several suggestions made
throughout this chapter.   The minimum standards are sum-
marized as follows:

> Recordings: 1,000 to 1,500 recordings in all
> audio formats; ten percent of recordings should
> be nonmusical; 500 discs, 500 tapes are minimum
> for beginning collection.
>
> Slides: 50 sets.
>
> Filmstrips: 50.
>
> Video Cassettes: 150 video cassettes for libraries
> serving over 50,000 population.
>
> 16mm Films: None (service areas with popula-
> tion under 25,000); membership in film circuit or
> cooperative recommended.
>
> Membership in a film circuit plus a small film
> collection of 25 to 50 titles (service areas with
> population of 25,000 to 50,000).
>
> One 16mm film print per 250 people (service
> areas with population over 50,000).
>
> 8mm Films: 100 (service areas with population
> over 25,000) (8mm film loops might also be con-
> sidered; content is largely structured for curricu-
> lum use.)

It is unwise to inaugurate a public service with less
than the recommended minimums.   Therefore, at first,
priorities by audiovisual format may have to be established.
A master plan for acquisitions should be formulated with
anticipated time frames specified.   (The Public Library Association's recommendations propose that budgeting permit
minimum standards to be reached within three years.)

A commitment by the library staff that an awareness
of the unique physical characteristics and communications

potential of AV media will also be a factor in the selection
procedure should be expressed somewhere in the policy.
This operating principle will be significant for librarians in
confronting actual workaday selection problems.
Let us assume, for example, that the same program
content is available in video cassette and 16mm film. The
easy access to all parts of the video cassette, with its fast
forward and rewind features, make the video cassette an excellent medium for autotutorial work in the library. However,
the shorter life of the tape, the unpredictable performance
of video playback equipment, and the limitation of audience
size because of video's typical small screen (except where
special equipment is used) are factors that have to be weighed
against the 16mm film's longer life, performance reliability,
easy repair and footage replacement, and versatility for large
or small groups or individuals, despite the 16mm film's accompanying shortcoming in regard to easy information retrieval. Only a review of the library's goals and special
community needs will provide assistance with such selection
problems.

In the aforementioned video cassette-16mm film selection case there is a not-so-obvious cost factor that is not
immediately apparent. At first glance it would seem that
the 16mm film's purchase price is perhaps six or more
times that of the video cassette for an equivalent amount of
running time. Not so, if the library intends to circulate
these materials to other library systems or educational institutions or organizations. Many videotapes are sold with
a condition that use be confined to the purchasing institution.
Sometimes generous copying privileges are allowed within
the institution. But when lending activity is likely to take
place outside the immediate jurisdiction of the purchaser,

special negotiations based on appropriately higher rates must
be worked out with the distributor.

There are some large distributors who offer expensive
production programming in videotape without circulation limitations but their initial charges are considerably higher and
restrictions of public advertising involving their videotapes
usually accompany the sale. The message here for librarians
is to read all contracts before buying, and to weigh factors
of purpose and cost.

No remarks in the hypothetical selection situation just
cited should be construed as anti-video cassette propaganda.
To even the score, it can be said that the video cassette is
most worthy of praise for its major role in a number of
recent library projects, particularly in dependent study work
at the high school equivalency and college levels. Indeed,
no library that purports to offer relevant public service today
can be without a video cassette collection.

The 16mm film requires special consideration in policy
making. Because some films may be leased for a period as
long as five years or may be rented for a short term, the
library with limited funds might ponder the possibility of
renting or leasing. Multiple showings of a rented film can
be arranged cooperatively among interested libraries on one
extended booking period, with a special rental fee worked
out with the distributor. This procedure is often used by
libraries to obtain certain films that are not for sale but are
only available by rental.

The selection policy should cite who is ultimately responsible for audiovisual materials selection and what role,
if any, committees will have in evaluating and selecting
materials. There are mixed opinions about committee participation and they will be discussed later on under "Evalu-

ation. " But whatever course is followed, "the buck" must
stop somewhere. A staff member involved with AV media
management should have the final say on what is ordered.

Not much is said about the library's archivist role in
regard to local history and related matters of local interest.
However, the PLA Recommendations statement goes out of
its way to stress the library's role in this regard.

> The library should work for the preservation and
> production of audiovisual resources, such as
> films, slides, and tapes of historic or other spe-
> cial value to its locality. Examples of such re-
> sources are films on cities or businesses of the
> region, slides showing land use resulting from
> highway department surveys, television films and
> tapes of events and personalities, and examples
> of work of local film producers. [4]

Audiovisual archives are not easily built. As suggested, the library should seek out what is being done locally. But just where materials are badly needed, appropriate
software for purchase is seldom to be found. Accordingly,
the staff should actively encourage local production. A good
photographer in the community might be willing to shoot and
sell slides to the library. Or a talented staff member could
be supplied with film to do the necessary work. A high
school or college is a possible source of videotapes and
audiotapes, and television stations will cooperate with libraries in dubbing locally produced programs merely for the
cost of the blank videotape to do the job. By the way, if
the library plans a major project in this field, it is important that historical societies in the area be consulted in
order to avoid redundant effort.

One last suggestion for the selection policy is to include a procedure for handling possible attempts to censor
audiovisual materials. Yes, people can become as incensed
about AV materials as they so often have about books, and

too frequently libraries are caught short with an inadequate
materials selection policy that fails to deal equally and fairly
with audiovisual media.   It is interesting how fast the staff's
fealty to the ALA Library Bill of Rights and related principles flies out of the window in the face of confrontations involving powerful media, such as 16mm films with their strong
visual and emotional impact.

Principles should be worked out in cooler, reasoned
times to serve later in the heat of crisis.   The policy also
ought to provide for a form, similar to that used for book
complaints, that is applicable to challenges of audiovisual
media.   The form ideally contains adequate space for the
patron to describe his or her experience with the material
in question and the reasons for requesting re-evaluation.

Obviously, all the philosophy and procedures recommended in the preceding remarks must be put in concise
written form with multiple copies easily accessible to the
public upon demand.   Samples of materials selection policy
statements incorporating AV media may be requested from
other libraries.

Selection Procedures

Once likely subjects and appropriate formats have
been determined through knowledge acquired about the public's needs and interests and the capabilities of various media, the search for appropriate titles begins.   Suggested
procedures to follow in that search are given below.

1.   Examine the reviews of various magazines devoted to
AV media.   Go back through several recent years' worth of
issues.   Some of the most likely sources are:

     The Booklist.   American Library Association, 50 E.
        Huron St., Chicago, Illinois 60611.

Published twice monthly, September through July, and once in August. Includes reviews of 16mm films, filmstrips, multimedia kits, nonmusical recordings (disc and cassette), and video cassettes.

Previews. R. R. Bowker Company, 1180 Avenue of the Americas, New York, N. Y. 10036.
Published monthly, September through May. Includes reviews of 16mm films, filmstrips, art prints, multimedia kits, and nonmusical recordings (disc and cassette).

Media & Methods. North American Publishing Company, 134 North American Building, 401 North Broad Street, Philadelphia, Pa. 19108.
Published nine times per year, September through May/ June. Each issue includes a few reviews of 16mm films, filmstrips, audio cassettes, and other media.

Film News. Film News Company, 250 West 57th St., Suite 2202. New York, N. Y. 10019.
Published bimonthly. Presents reviews of 16mm films, including feature-length theatrical films, and filmstrips.

Hi Fidelity/Musical America. Billboard Publications, Great Barrington, Mass. 01230.
Published monthly. Includes reviews and lists of musical recordings, discs and audio tapes.

Hi Fi/Stereo Review. Ziff-Davis Publishing Co. , 1 Park Ave. , New York, N. Y. 10016.
Published monthly. Reviews stereophonic musical discs and audio tapes.

2. Subscribe to a 16mm film evaluation service, such as:

EFLA Evaluations. Educational Film Library Association, Inc. , 16 W. 60 St. , New York, N. Y. 10023.
A continuous service throughout the year. Provides motion picture reviews on 3" by 5" cards. Evaluates over 300 titles annually. Available only to members. Apply for membership and cost information.

Landers Film Reviews. Landers Associates, P. O. Box 69760, Los Angeles, Calif. 90069.
Published monthly during the year except June, July and August. Gives evaluations for nontheatrical films. Provides a handy index for each volume published.

3. Search for reviews of likely titles in special indexes, such as:

> International Index to Multi-Media Information. Audio-Visual Associates, 186 East California Blvd. , Pasadena, Calif. 91105.
> Gives name of periodical, date and page number, plus brief evaluative quote from review cited. Provides grade range audience levels. With separate subject and title sections, lists of magazines and distributors.

> Notes. Music Library Association, Research Library of the Performing Arts, 111 Amsterdam Avenue, New York, N. Y. 10023.
> Published quarterly. Indexes reviews of recordings found in many periodicals with symbol indication of favorable or unfavorable reviews.

4. Send for, and keep on hand, an assortment of audiovisual materials catalogs from other U. S. libraries. It is a common practice for public libraries to exchange catalogs, but, if necessary, copies may be purchased. A list of addresses of major public libraries appears in The Bowker Annual of Library and Book Trade Information (R. R. Bowker Co. , 1180 Avenue of the Americas, New York, N. Y. 10036).

5. Look up published subject bibliographies of audiovisual materials (alternately known as mediographies, filmographies, discographies, et al.). Check the purpose and scope of such lists for applicability before using.

6. Search for possible titles in various indexes (or source guides) such as those listed before. (Note: listings in these sources do not indicate quality of materials. Previewing before purchase may be necessary.)

FILMS (16mm)

> NICEM Index to 16mm Educational Films. National Information Center for Educational Media, University of Southern California, University Park, Los Angeles, Calif. 90007.
> A guide to 16mm educational motion pictures. Has subject guide, title section with complete descriptive data, and list of distributors.

Educators Guide to Free Films. Educators Progress
Service, Randolph, Wisconsin 53956.
Published annually. A listing of sponsored free films by
subject and title. Provides sources.

FILMSTRIPS

NICEM Index to 35mm Filmstrips. National Information
Center for Educational Media, University of Southern
California, University Park, Los Angeles, Calif.
90007.
A guide to 35mm filmstrips. Has subject guide, title
section with complete descriptive data, and list of distributors.

Educators Guide to Free Filmstrips. Educators Progress
Service, Randolph, Wisconsin, 53956.
Published annually. A listing of sponsored free films by
subject and title. Provides sources.

SLIDES

NICEM Index to Educational Slides. National Information
Center for Educational Media, University of Southern
California, University Park, Los Angeles, Calif.
90007.
A guide to commercially produced slides. Has subject
guide, title main entry section with complete descriptive
data, and list of distributors.

RECORDINGS

NICEM Index to Educational Audio Tapes. National In-
formation Center for Educational Media, University of
Southern California, University Park, Los Angeles,
Calif. 90007.
A guide to commercially produced educational audio tapes.
Has subject guide, title section with complete descriptive
data, and list of distributors.

Schwann Record and Tape Guide. W. W. Schwann, 137
Newbury St. , Boston, Mass. 02116.
Published monthly. Lists stereo recordings (discs and
audiotapes) currently available. Mostly musical recordings, but includes some nonmusical items as well.

FILMS (8mm)

NICEM Index to 8mm Motion Cartridges. National Information Center for Educational Media, University
   of Southern California, University Park, Los Angeles,
   Calif. 90007.
A guide to commercially produced 8mm loop cartridges.
Has subject guide, title section with complete descriptive
data, and list of distributors.

VIDEOTAPES

NICEM Index to Educational Videotapes. National Information Center for Educational Media, University
   of Southern California, University Park, Los Angeles,
   Calif. 90007.
Includes tapes in reel-to-reel format and cassettes of
various specifications from 1/2" to 2". (The 3/4" format is the one generally used by public libraries.) The
guide contains a subject section, title section with complete descriptive data, and list of distributors.

The Video Bluebook. Knowledge Industry Publications,
   Inc., 2 Corporate Park Drive, Dept. 429K, White
   Plains, N.Y. 10602.
A compendium of video services and programs. Lists
video "publishers" and over 2,000 programs. Also con-
tains a subject arrangement of titles and series.

MISCELLANEOUS MEDIA

Films and Other Materials for Projection. Library of
   Congress, Catalog Publication Division of the Processing Dept., Washington, D.C.
Includes title and subject listings of audiovisual materials
for projection (motion pictures, filmstrips, sets of transparencies, and slide sets) currently cataloged by the Library of Congress. Serves as an acquisition and reference tool since annotations and full descriptive cataloging are provided for each item. Published in three
quarterly issues (Jan-Mar, Apr-June, July-Sept) with annual and quinquennial cumulations. May also be obtained
on 3" by 5" printed cards mailed to subscribers on a
monthly basis.

7.   Locate potentially useful titles in distributors' catalogs.
A collection of catalogs should be built up. Names and ad-

dresses of major companies can be obtained from the lists
of distributors and producers that appear in the works cited
in sections 2 and 6 above.   Another good general source of
distributor information is Audiovisual Marketplace: A Multi
Media Guide (R. R. Bowker Company, 1180 Avenue of the
Americas, New York, N. Y. 10036).   This is an annual publication that, among many other kinds of information, gives
lists of producers and distributors classified by media and
subject.

Here are a few sources of distribution for media less easy
to find:

Center for Cassette Studies, 8110 Webb Ave. , North
Hollywood, Calif. 91605; issues a catalog of audio text
cassettes.   (Note: purchaser buys one copy and makes
as many cassette copies as needed.)

National Center for Audio Tapes, University of Colorado,
Stadium Building, Boulder, Colorado 80302; issues a
catalog with subject and alphabetical title listings.   (Note:
many tapes are available for purchase with unlimited use
rights.)

The Public Television Library, 475 L'Enfant Plaza, S.
W. , Washington, D. C. 20024; issues videocassete program catalog with listings of informative, entertainment,
and educational television programming produced by public television stations across the U. S.   (Most programs
are available in 3/4" cassette format, although some
programs may also be obtainable in 2" and 16mm film
formats.)

Local public television stations are also good sources of
videotapes not listed in the Public Television Library's
catalog.

Reel-to-reel 8mm entertainment films can be obtained
from sources such as Blackhawk Films, Davenport,
Iowa.

College Art Association of America publishes an annotated listing of art slide sources in the U. S. and throughout the world (Slide Buyers Guide); available from Nancy
DeLaurier, Curator of Slides and Photographs, Dept. of
Art and Art History, University of Missouri, Kansas
City, Mo. 64110.   This booklet also gives some comments
about the general quality of slides from various sources.

Reviews for titles under consideration should be consulted whenever possible. Otherwise previewing is recommended.

A word of warning about AV media reviews should be given. Reviews vary in quality and scope--much more so than reviews of books, for example. Some audiovisual reviews are merely descriptive, others give evaluations in depth. The librarian, through trial and error, will learn to distinguish what is most helpful. However, there comes a time when the librarian finds that even the so-called "best" reviews prove to be inadequate for the library's purposes. The number of titles of various formats covered is not as ample as desired. Reviewers often fail to bring sufficient imagination and flexibility to the evaluation process, particularly in regard to the potential use factor--one of the more important evaluative criteria for AV materials. The result of these shortcomings is a manifest need to preview materials in advance of purchase.

The previewing of films and filmstrips is easy to arrange. Most distributors will be happy to send preview copies of their titles, and sometimes they will even agree to ship "purchase" prints which may be retained with a confirming order after a favorable evaluation. However, other media, particularly musical recordings, are more difficult to get in advance of purchase. The situation for educational tapes and discs and videotapes is a little better, but irregular. When in doubt, the librarian should write the dealer and ask about the policy.

Evaluation

Certain foreseeable difficulties can be minimized if distinction is made between the evaluation and selection processes. It is helpful for the librarian in charge of

audiovisual services to be able to call on individual staff
members for help in previewing and evaluation. And, of
course, staff suggestions for purchase should always be wel-
come. However, in the eyes of many experienced audiovisual librarians the role of committee in evaluation is a
mixed blessing. Ideally, all staff should become familiar
with AV resources. [5]

When a group gets together, there is an obligation to
decide on, endorse, or rule on something, either unanimous-
ly or by majority. And when the group has decreed that a
certain item is "approved" for purchase, the actual message is--"buy it!" In other words evaluation has slipped
over into selection.

Some will wonder about this questioning of committee
participation. The reason for it lies in the lack of perspec-
tive and uneven background of participants, combined with
the special problems of AV evaluation and the special need
in AV acquisition for a high value return for money and
effort expended. Many "print" librarians view nonprint media in terms of potential usefulness in the library's programs and special projects rather than on the basis of how
the patrons would want to utilize the materials for their own
needs.

On the other hand, assuming that the library truly
desires committee participation and has clearly delineated
the roles of such committees in evaluation, staff members
can most comfortably be recruited to evaluation groups that
are organized by public service age level categories, i. e. ,
adult, children's, young adult.

The librarian in charge of audiovisual services should
not hesitate to ask the patrons what they want and to involve
them sometimes in the evaluation process. This is particu-

larly beneficial in subject areas in which special expertise is required, e.g., technical subjects, ethnic cultures, and the like. An added dividend is the improved good will this kind of involvement can bring.

Evaluation Criteria

All librarians are trained in general principles of evaluation. Therefore no master list of guidelines needs to be given here. Instead, the application of what is already known to AV materials reviewing can be indicated.

Criteria vary according to the kinds of materials being evaluated, the conditions under which the material will be used, the needs of the community and the library's goals (factors already examined with examples in the discussion of "Policy"). Customary concerns of accuracy, scope, style, intelligibility, and the like must be broadened to allow examination of certain AV considerations: technical production values (color, sound, editing, focus, composition), artistic values (originality, imaginative treatment, realization of artistic goals), and physical features (durability, convenience, attractiveness, possibilities for utilization).

As for book evaluation, it is customary to have a form on which the reviewer's remarks can be written. There is a wide range of models. For example, an elaborate, detailed instrument is used by most film festivals, e.g., the American Film Festival of the Educational Film Library Association. Or a simple little 3" by 5" slip of paper (sample submitted by one public library given below) or forms of intermediate complexity will do.

```
Film title_____ Min. _____

Age level: Adult__ 12-16 yrs. __ 6-11 yrs. __ Preschool__
Evaluation: Poor__ Fair__ Good__ Very Good__ Excellent__
General impression of film:  (use back if needed)



Name_____ Organization_____
Address_____ Tel No. _____ Date_____
```

A time-saving practice is to have the audiovisual
staff write up descriptive data and an annotation suitable for
use in cataloging on whatever form is employed.

Above all, inexperienced librarians assigned to examine AV materials for purchase should be on guard against
a certain passivity that seems to take over in the acts of
listening and/or viewing. Influenced perhaps by past experience limited almost exclusively to the spectator's role in
contacts with AV media, fledgling reviewers must make an
effort to become active, judicious evaluators.

Organization

The big question in organizing audiovisual materials
is to decide which way is best to serve the public and yet
will make it convenient for the staff to render that service?
The possibilities are numerous. However, the easiest and
simplest will be emphasized, with the smaller public library
in mind.

Existing plans for physical arrangement of AV media
reflect several different approaches. Probably the most
common scheme in public libraries is for the nonprint collection to be separated from, but adjacent to, the print

materials. Another possibility is to have a separate audiovisual section or department. A newer treatment (pioneered
in school media centers and college libraries but an innova-
tion as yet in public libraries) is an "integration" approach
which calls for placement of AV media on open shelves side
by side with the books. A few exceptions are made for formats of unusual shape or size, e. g., discs, which are
shelved in separate shelves or racks located as close as
possible to the print materials. And some ingenious solutions have been devised in packaging and shelving modifications to bring the various media together for easy access by
the patron. Some of these ideas will be discussed in later
comments about audiovisual materials.

An equally important question--to classify or not to
classify, and its corollary, which treatment is best for cataloging AV media?--is closely allied with physical location.
The integrated materials plan just referred to absolutely requires classification and cataloging of a style comparable to
that for books, and the library's catalog will likewise inte-
grate all print and nonprint materials by title and subject.
If the small library decides instead to use one of the other
organization schemes, it may consider several options in
classification and cataloging depending on taste and available
funds. Such options and related matters are discussed in
the following section in which the different audiovisual media
are examined one by one. However, it should be stressed
that the PLA Recommendations encourage that all library resources be included in a catalog of some sort.

16mm Films

16mm films are usually kept in a separate section or
department of the library because of the problems of their

care and maintenance and special methods of circulating
them. Since films are most frequently reserved or "booked"
for specific show dates, special circulation records or "cal-
endars" are kept for each print in the collection. A multiple
copy form for reservations should be devised for patron requests. One copy usually serves for confirmation to the
patron, another is for the circulation file, another for shipment or date due information, and others as needed, depending on information desired.

Packaging and storage of films are interdependent.
If films are classified or otherwise grouped by subject (perhaps with color coding) they are usually kept in film cans in
special steel shelving equipped with racks that hold individual
cans of varied circumferences side by side in vertical position. When films housed in this manner are loaned, they
are placed inside a two-piece fiberboard shipping case (cans
with reels). One copy of the reservation form is placed in
the 4" by 6" frame on the outside of the case lid.

If the library chooses to use the newer heavy duty
plastic film cases which serve both shipping and shelving
functions, extra steps and the need for special shelving can
be eliminated. These cases are designed to stand up on
their own without support, and, once in its case, a film
doesn't have to be repacked in another container for shipment. Deep adjustable shelving of any sort can be employed,
with film storage arranged by reel size (400, 600, 800, 1200,
1600 and 2000 feet being the common 16mm film sizes) and
in alphabetical order by titles lettered on the sides of cases.
No classification is necessary with this method. However,
reservation and shipment procedure is the same as with the
other method, as the plastic cases also have a 4" by 6"
frame outside the case to hold the reservation or circulation
form.

Because patrons who regularly use motion pictures
often need to plan for screenings or programs for others
(family, friends, clubs, classes, and other kinds of audiences), film cataloging can probably be handled most conveniently in a separate book catalog which is offered to the
public for sale at a minimal cost. In this way frequent film
borrowers are able to schedule film showings from their
homes or offices, using their own catalog copies to select
and order the films.

8mm Films

8mm films (reel to reel or loops) can be treated like
books in an integrated arrangement because of the nature
and size of the cardboard containers in which they are sold.
They may also be shelved separately. If the former is the
case, classification is essential.

A mystik tape hinge applied to one side of the box
lid helps to secure the lid to the bottom of the box in situations in which the two-part box is used for packaging.
Lettering or written labels can be applied to the side of
each 8mm film container to facilitate identification in vertical shelving arrangements.

Some libraries treat 8mm film as the paperbacks of
the film world, spending little time or effort on their technical processing or repair. Also, cataloging effort is minimized and brief lists of titles available are offered in lieu
of cataloging. As indicated earlier, however, regardless
of other factors, such as shelving, packaging, and so on,
all library resources should be described in a catalog of
some sort.

Filmstrips
<hr />

 Filmstrips are sold in small cans with lids and are often stored in special cabinets with drawers equipped with special dividers to hold the filmstrip cans in place. Unfortunately, with this method the discs or cassettes that accompany "sound" filmstrips must be stored separately and the two parts brought together upon patron request. An alternate method, in which filmstrips with their discs or cassettes are packaged in cardboard containers available from various library supply houses, permits faster and more convenient public service.

 If the latter method is used, filmstrips can be shelved like books on shelves, either separately or in an integrated organizational scheme. As mentioned elsewhere, classification is of course necessary when the integrated plan is adopted. Filmstrips shelved separately could be arranged quite simply in alphabetical order by title, if classification is not required. Cataloging could be integrated with the library's print materials catalog, or, if a film catalog in book form exists, placed with the cataloging of other audiovisual materials there.

 Some libraries lately have been putting filmstrips or filmstrips and cassettes in sets in transparent plastic "hang up" bags which are arranged on rods attached to shelves. This method can be used for filmstrip collections in which each shelf has been provided with a hang-up bag rod to bring filmstrips in close proximity with other media of the same subject. If hanging filmstrips are to be stored separately, they may be arranged alphabetically by title or classified. Whenever possible, classification is preferred.

Slides

Slides can be placed in slide boxes designed to hold sets, or slipped into slots of slide show "pages" which in turn are put into heavy duty expanding envelopes along with bound scripts that describe each slide in the set. A third possibility can be adopted when slides are combined with cassettes in kits, in which the slides are stored in Kodak Carousel slide trays that in turn are placed in a two-piece cardboard box along with the accompanying cassette.

Slides, handled as described above in the first two instances, are best stored separately on shelves. With the second method of packaging another alternative is to place the expanding envelopes alphabetically by title in filing cabinet drawers.

Classification options for slides are the same as those presented for filmstrips.

Video Cassettes

Video cassettes come in cases that almost look like books. Shelving them with books in an integrated collection is obviously quite easy. Video cassettes may also be maintained in separate shelving. Whatever is done, vertical storage is preferred. Video cassettes are not to be stacked horizontally for long periods of time. Manufacturers warn of the drop-out of magnetic oxide particles from the tape in horizontal storage.

Classification options are the same for video cassettes as for filmstrips.

Recordings

Audio tape cassettes can be put in special cardboard

boxes obtainable from most library supply houses. With this
type of packaging cassettes may be given a shelf treatment
like books.

Audio tape cassettes can also be placed in plastic
hang-up bags as in the last suggestion cited for filmstrips.
Shelving can be separate or integrated--again as suggested
for filmstrips.

Another treatment of audio tape cassettes is to place
them in specially designed large drawers which hold cassettes
in order.

Classification options for audio tape cassettes are the
same as those presented for filmstrips, and the cautions re-
garding vertical storage as made for video cassettes hold
also for audio tape cassettes.

Phono discs are too large for the integrated shelving
approach. Therefore, libraries most frequently arrange
discs on shelves with dividers that keep phonograph discs
standing straight. Another common practice is putting discs
in browser bins.

Classification of discs is preferred, as for all media,
but some libraries have devised an inordinate variety of ways
besides classification, perhaps because librarians have been
working with discs for a longer number of years. Some alternate methods used: by accession number, by manufacturer's number, by broad subject area arrangement (with color
codes or letter notation as location symbols), or in alphabetical order by composer, author or title.

The organizational ideas given throughout the preceding
pages have been culled from actual practice in libraries
throughout the U. S. The simplest solutions have been frankly
revealed in an earnest effort to encourage as many public libraries as possible to inaugurate audiovisual services for

their communities. For although the more elaborate methods may be preferred, as immediate guidelines they sometimes stifle rather than inspire first steps into the audiovisual world. Let the initial goal instead be maximum service with minimal endeavor.

Notes

1. Public Library Association. Recommendations for Audiovisual Materials and Services for Small and Medium-Sized Public Libraries. American Library Association, 1975, p. 14.

2. Ibid., pp. 14-15.   3. Ibid., pp. 14-16.

4. Ibid., p. 16.   5. Ibid., p. 13.

6. Ibid., p. 12.

Chapter 2

AUDIOVISUAL HARDWARE

by Leon L. Drolet, Jr.

The selection of audio-visual hardware for use by the
public library patron is often influenced by the kind and the
number of audiovisual playback units already owned and in
use by the general public. When a library begins to establish an audiovisual service, since it is most familiar with
consumer product lines such as General Electric, Magnavox,
RCA, and Zenith, it tends to select consumer products in
an attempt to satisfy the library's audiovisual needs. Unfortunately, most consumer products are not designed to withstand the heavy use and the abuse experienced in a library
setting. As a result, equipment failure and rapid deprecia-
tion are common occurrences.

A complete audiovisual product line has, however,
been designed to satisfy the heavy demands placed on hardware used in industry, schools, and public libraries. The
Audio-Visual Equipment Directory[1] is the "Yellow Pages" of
industrial/educational grade audiovisual hardware. It lists
not only the kinds of equipment but specific manufacturers'
models, along with the names and addresses of the dealers
and manufacturers offering equipment.

Upon inspection of this directory, the librarian will
notice that the design of industrial/educational audiovisual

26

equipment is simple and lacks the cosmetics normally associated with home products. The internal workings of hardware for industry and schools also tend to be simple. Manufacturers believe that as a piece of hardware becomes in-
creasingly complex, the greater is the likelihood of an equipment failure. To further insure the reliability of their product, many manufacturers use "heavy duty" motors, gears,
and parts. These precautions are not deemed necessary in
the case of consumer products which normally experience
casual use.

AUDIO HARDWARE

Phonograph Record Players

Most libraries begin offering audiovisual services with
the provision of phonograph records. The audio disc still
remains the most commonly owned audiovisual piece of software among the public; as a result, most households own one
or more phonograph record players.

In many libraries, two unique phonograph record collections develop. One is designed to meet the adult patron's
requirements, the other is earmarked for the child patron.
Just as the collections are different, the hardware required
to provide the playback of phonograph records found in the
adult area is unlike that located in the children's section.

Story hour and other children's programs at times require group listening, and thus a phonograph player with a
loudspeaker is desirable. For individual listening, 'the speaker
in all phonographs is disconnected electronically whenever a
headset plug is inserted into the proper receptacle.

It is interesting to note that the majority of the recordings produced for the youngster are monaural. To be

pragmatic as well as adhere to the philosophy previously
stated--that the simpler a device is, the less is the chance
that it will break--a monaurel record player with a stereo
compatible stylus will adequately meet the demands of the
children's department.

The Audiotronics Corporation, Califone International
Incorporated, Hamilton Electronics Corporation, Newcomb
Audio Products Company, and V-M Corporation offer the
largest variety of phonograph record players for the public
library. Upon inspection, the librarian will notice the great
similarity between the product lines offered by the manufacturers. These companies purchase the major components
from the same suppliers. The main difference between the
manufacturers and their various models are found in the
amount of audio output power, size of loudspeaker, and the
packaging. Large audio output power (wattage) as well as
large speakers add to the price of a player.

The Audio-Visual Accessories and Supplies model,
AV-10T, priced at $125.00; Audiotronics model, ATC-300E,
at $84.95; Califone model, 14300, at $117.00; GHV Electronics model, RP110, at $86.95; Hamilton model, Mighty 920,
at $87.90; MPC Educational Systems Incorporated model,
Pause Master MRP-111-P, at $89.95; McClure Projectors
Incorporated model, X-101, at $79.95; Newcomb model, EDT-
28C, at $89.95; V-M Corporation model, 275-7AV, at $84.90;
and the Valiant Instructional Materials Corporation model, AV-
125T, at $69.50, are good units for group and individual lis-
tening in the public library's children's section. There is
not a clear "winner" among these players and the local
dealer's ability to repair any of these units should enter into
consideration when a library is selecting a player.

The use of the phonograph record player by the adult

patron, for the most part, is on an individual basis, requiring the use of a headset in lieu of a loudspeaker. Stereophonic reproduction is desirable since most adult and young adult recordings of music are binaural.

The number of stereophonic phonograph record players designed for industrial/educational use is limited. The Audiotronics model, 340ST, priced at $179.95; Califone model, 1130K, at $183.00; Hamilton model, 942, at $157.80; MP Audio Corporation model, PT95, at $142.95; and Newcomb model, EDTS-40, at $169.95, are able to meet the listening needs of the public library patron. All of these units except for the MP Audio PT 95, come with detachable speakers. [2] Some of the manufacturers allow the return of the loudspeakers for credit if the library feels that the purchased unit will be used exclusively for headset listening. All of these models are table-top units and the overall quality of reproduction is equal, with a slight edge in favor of the MP Audio PT 95 for headset only use.

For aesthetic reasons many public libraries prefer the flush mounting of audiovisual equipment into table or carrel tops. Properly mounted units can retard theft attempts. There are available security locks for table-top units which perform the same task of impeding theft but these locks distract from the aesthetic impact of audiovisual playback units.

Currently, no flush-mounted phonograph record player with a built-in amplifier for headsets is offered by the manufacturers of industrial/educational audiovisual products. Califone International does offer a special kit to enable many of its record players to be flush mounted. An alternate to the modification of the Califone players is the combination of a Shure Brothers Incorporated Solo-Phone amplifier with

a turntable model ARXB manufactured by Acoustic Research
Incorporated and a magnetic stereo cartridge model 500E
produced by Stanton Magnetics Incorporated. An alternate to
the Stanton cartridge is the Shure SC35C stereo cartridge.
This combination of components has a total selling price of
$180. 00. Of all the stereo phonograph record players listed,
the component package built around the Solo-Phone headset
amplifier provides the best in sound reproduction.

8-Track Audio Cartridge Players

The second most common audio-visual software format owned by the general public is the 8-track audio cartridge, which contains a continuous loop of magnetic recording tape. While the consumer has purchased in large quantities the pre-recorded 8-track format, industry and educational institutions have not utilized the format. As a result,
no heavy duty 8-track playback unit is manufactured.

Libraries wishing to offer 8-track format will have
to purchase a consumer unit offered by such manufacturers
as General Electric, JVC America, Lafayette Radio Electronics Corporation, Panasonic, and Sony. By connecting
an 8-track tape deck selling for approximately $80. 00 with
an industrial/educational grade headphone amplifier, Shure
Solo-Phone, which sells for $55. 00, satisfactory sound repro-
duction can be realized.

Audio Cassette Players

The audio cassette containing magnetic recording tape
has been widely accepted by the consumer as well as by industry and educational institutions. Even though the cassette
was primarily designed for the recording of the human voice,

as a result of the development of new kinds of recording
tapes and the careful redesigning of the internal workings of
the cassette player, high quality reproduction of music is
possible.

Due to its relatively small size and its ability to record information, the audio cassette offers great flexibility
in the ways in which it may be used as a part of public library service. Battery-operated portable cassette players
enable any location within or outside the library to become a
listening post. A number of cassette units produced for in-
dustrial/educational utilization offer a playback only function.
They can be operated either on batteries or alternating current (AC). These units produce monophonic sound whether
or not the cassette has been recorded in a stereophonic format.

Not unlike monaural phonograph record players, the
main differences between various models is the audio output
power and the size of the speaker. Unlike the record player,
there are a variety of different features available and each
cassette unit comprises a combination of these features.
The most attractive portable cassette players will have a
built-in AC power adaptor, thus eliminating the need for an
external AC adaptor kit, which is prone to breakage. Detachable AC power cords tend, due to human nature, to become misplaced; therefore a power cord permanently attached
to the cassette player is preferred if there is a storage
place within the unit for the chord when operating under bat-
tery power. Push-button controls regulating the fast-forward,
play, rewind, and stop functions of the tape transport system
are desirable, rather than a single lever control regulating
these tape movement functions. A button-controlled eject
system which lifts the dust cover and pops up the cassette

for easy removal is favored over a manually lifted dust cover
which, again due to human nature, tends to be raised too
far, resulting in broken hinges. The Califone model 3500, priced at $59.95, is the
only cassette player free from the design shortcomings listed
in the previous paragraph. The Audiotronics model, 146,
priced at $49.95; Bell and Howell model, 3070, at $44.95;
and the Viewlex Audio-Visual model, CP-3, at $59.95, will
serve well in public library service. The economy-minded
library might consider the Hitachi Sales Corporation of America model, TPQ 202, at $29.95, or the MPC Educational
Systems Incorporated model, CS-202E, at $24.95. The
Hitachi TPQ 202 has an established record for providing
faithful service to those libraries which circulate cassette
players to the patron for home use.

There are AC-only powered monaural cassette players for table-top use or for flush mounting into a carrel or
table top. These units are well suited to the playback of
children's material. Most of the pre-recorded tapes for
children are in the monaural format. The only flush-mounted
AC-operated monaural cassette playback unit is manufactured
by the Wollensak/3M Company. Its model 2505 AV is priced
at $170.00 and is an excellent unit which has proven itself
to be quite durable.

Table-top AC-only powered monaural cassette players
may come equipped with a loudspeaker for group listening,
as would be required during a children's or adult library
program. The Califone model, 3650, at $140.00, or the
Wollensak/3M model, 2610AV, at $140.00, can be used for
individual as well as group listening. If the library plans
to use the cassette player for large audiences, the Califone
3650 has a high-power amplifier to meet group listening

Leon L. Drolet, Jr.   33

requirements. For small groups and individual use, the
Wollensak is preferred.

The adult patron will prefer the stereophonic playback
of audio cassettes. The MP Audio Corporation model, PC-
97, priced at $153.45, is the only table-top stereo cassette
player designed for exclusive headset use. There is no in-
dustrial/educational grade stereo table top cassette player
on the market offering sound reproduction through loudspeak-
ers.

The only flush-mounted AC stereo cassette playback
unit manufactured is the Telex Communications Incorporated
model, 155. This model comprises a separate tape deck
and an amplifier able to drive one headset. In order to
flush mount the Telex 155, two cutouts in a table top are
required. Another setback to the Telex unit is that the
cassette eject system often fails to completely pop up the
cassette for easy removal.

An alternate to the Telex unit is the Wollensak model,
2516AV, stereo cassette deck which is very easy to use and
offers excellent fidelity. This unit, however, has the ability
to record, which could present a threat to the pre-recorded
cassette. An audiovisual dealer can easily defeat the record
function of this unit. The Wollensak 2516AV sells for
$260.00.

Reel-to-Reel Tape Recorder/Playback Units

Tape recorders are required to capture on magnetic
tape library programs, board meetings, local events of historical or general interest, and oral history. If the library
seeks professional recordings, a reel-to-reel tape recorder
should be utilized. While a stereophonic model might add
some degree of realism, a library should utilize a monaural

unit since it requires less critical microphone placement
than a stereo model and monophonic tapes are easier to edit.
The Sony model, TC106AV, priced at $279.95, or the
Wollensak model, 1520AV, at $230.00, will meet public li-
brary needs. The Sony TC106AV offers three record/play-
back speeds (1-7/8 ips, 3-3/4 ips, 7-1/2 ips), as compared
with the Wollensak 1520AV's two speeds (3-3/4 ips, 7-1/2
ips). However, the construction, durability, and quality of
the Wollensak make it more attractive than the Sony.

Reel-to-reel magnetic tape is fragile and most librarians do not offer this format for patron use. If the library desires to make available reel-to-reel listening facilities, the Crown International model, SP722, priced at $795.00,
is a semi-professional playback-only unit designed to be
flush mounted and is able to take abuse. It is very easy to
thread and operate.

Cassette Tape Recorder/Playback Units

A portable cassette record/playback unit offers adequate recording of events. These units are less expensive
than reel-to-reel tape recorders. There are many good cassette recorders made for the consumer market which will
perform satisfactorily for library staff use.

Portable cassette recorders generally fall within three
price ranges: $15 to $40, $60 to $90, and $100 up. The
essential differences between the low and medium priced units
are the drive and transport system and the sophistication of
the electronics. The more expensive units tend to be more
attractive in appearance and offer features such as compact
design and monitor meters to assist in making quality recordings.

A cassette record/player unit priced in the $60 to $90
area will provide satisfactory service. The differences be-

tween the competitive brands are insignificant. By selecting
a name brand such as General Electric, Panasonic, J. C.
Penney, Sears, Sony, Wards, etc. the library will purchase
a good unit with good product support enabling the unit to be
repaired within a reasonable time period and price.
Libraries which prefer recording on audio cassette in
situations where the portability of the machine is not a key
factor have the opportunity to select from many table-top
models which are AC powered. The Audiotronics model,
160, at $179. 95; Avid Corporation model, 910, at $190. 00;
Califone model, 3670, at $200. 00; Newcomb model, EDC-100,
at $199. 95; Sharp model, AV2000, at $159. 95; Telex model,
529, at $229. 95; and the Wollensak model, 2520AV, at $210. 00,
can adequately record as well as reproduce library material. All of these units come supplied with a loudspeaker
and high-power amplifiers. The Avid 910 comes with a
built-in microphone which might prove convenient but which
offers a lower quality recording. The Wollensak has an excellent tape transport system which will offer many hours of
trouble-free operation. The Audiotronics 160 and Califone
3650 offer a review cue feature which will assist a library
in transcribing tapes.

Cassette Recorder/Player with Built-in Synchronizer

A filmstrip projector or a slide projector with semi-
automatic image advance can be kept automatically in time
with recorded material by a cassette recorder/player with a
built-in synchronizer. An inaudible signal (pulse) is recorded at the command of the operator on the cassette along
with the sound track. The pulse is read back in the playback mode and triggers the changing of the visual at the
correct place in the recorded program.

As with standard cassette record/playback units, the
audio output power (wattage) and the size of the speaker influence the selling price of a unit. The number of inaudible
commands as well as the kind of signal are also reflected in
the cost.

There are two kinds of signals: the 50 Hertz superimposed pulse, used mainly for filmstrip programs, and the
pulse recorded on a separate track, which is used for the
majority of slide programs. Two separate functions can be
controlled by pulses recorded on a separate track. They
are advance and pulse/stop. The ability of the cassette
playback system to differentiate between types of pulses and
to recognize a pulse among recorded material or residual
noise left on the tape also influences the selling price of the
unit.

Playback-only units, for patron use, which are able
to control projectors are the Beacon model, TP-300V, from
Whitehouse Products Incorporated, priced at $120.00; Buhl
Projector Company model, 1000, at $150.00; Optisonics Hec
Corporation model, Sound-O-Matic Educator Playback 10-
6301-01, at $299.00; T. M. Visual Industries Incorporated
model, TMC 25W, at $119.95; and V-M Corporation model,
752AV, at $79.00. While the V-M 752AV lacks push-button
controls to regulate the functions of the tape transport, it
still remains the most attractive playback unit. The Opti-
sonics 10-6301-01 is a universal playback unit able to read
both superimposed as well as separate track pulses, thus
enabling it to operate both a slide projector and a filmstrip
projector in an automatic function.

Playback cassette models only able to control the advance on semi-automatic filmstrip projectors are the Avid
model, 505, at $149.50; Bell and Howell model, 3025, at

$57. 95; and Optisonic model, Sound-O-Matic Educator Play-
back 10-6301-01, at $299. 00.   The Bell and Howell 3025
will meet small group listening requirements; the Avid 505
performs better for large groups.

Record/playback cassette players with built-in synch-
ronizers for public library staff use in constructing a tape/
slide program are the Audiotronic model, 152S, at $149. 95;
Beacon model, TRPS-650, at $175. 00; Buhl model, 1000, at
$159. 95; Optisonics model, Sound-O-Matic 1, at $219. 95;
Sony model, Pitchman, at $399. 95; V-M Corporation model,
756AV, at $225. 00; and the Wollensak model, 2551AV Por-
table, at $340. 00.   All these units permit the recording of
a sound track as well as adding or erasing of a pulse to advance the slide projector to the next slide.   The Optisonic's
Sound-O-Matic 1 is recommended for individual or small
group listening, while the Sony "Pitchman" or the Wollensak
2551AV will satisfy larger group needs.

The Optisonic model, Sound-O-Matic V, at $289. 00;
Telex model, C-130, at $424. 95, and Wollensak model,
2570AV, at $390. 00, allow the programmer to control the
advance of the slide as well as to place a pulse command
to pause/stop the tape program to permit discussion.   The
Sound-O-Matic V is good for smaller groups; the Wollensak
will satisfy larger groups.

The Radmar Incorporated model, 505 Porta-Pak, at
$150. 00, permits the superimposed recording of a pulse
required for most filmstrip playback systems.

Audio Cassette High Speed Duplicators

To protect and extend the life of a pre-recorded cassette, some public libraries have generated from the original
tape a copy which is to be circulated to the library patron.

In order not to violate the copyright law, these libraries
have acquired duplication rights from the copyright holder.

To reduce the time to duplicate the contents recorded
on an audio cassette, a high-speed cassette tape duplicator
is required. The so-called "cassette copier" is designed
for repeated and heavy use. Most public libraries will require a copier which can reproduce stereophonic cassette
tape masters.

Cassette copiers differ in the rate of speed of dupli-
cating a tape, the ability to erase a cassette onto which new
information is to be recorded, and the automatic rewinding
of the cassette at the end of the record cycle. The International Audio Incorporated model, Alpha 41, priced at
$1295.00, and the Pentagon Industries Incorporated model,
Super C4, at $1195.00, duplicate all four tracks of a stereo
cassette in a single pass. These are the fastest copiers,
requiring less than two minutes to duplicate a cassette with
a total playing time of sixty minutes (30 minutes per side).
The Telex model, Cassette Copier IV, priced at $1395.00,
is able to duplicate a sixty-minute cassette in just over
three minutes, while the Recordex Corporation model, Duplicator I, at $999.95, requires four minutes to record a sixty-
minute tape.

There are other cassette copiers which operate at
slower speeds but if the public library plans to offer "on
demand" copying, four minutes would seem the maximum that
a patron would be willing to wait. The waiting period could
be quite long if more than one cassette were requested.

The International Audio Incorporated Alpha 41 is the
best constructed of the available copiers and should prove
the most reliable. The Pentagon C4 or Recordex I are able
to satisfy most public library needs. Regardless of the unit

selected, the library will be required to purchase a bulk tape eraser in order to "clean" the recycled cassettes which already have recorded information on them.

VIDEO HARDWARE

16mm Motion Picture Projectors

The basic design of the 16mm projector has not changed in the past thirty years. Recently, there have been refinements that make the 16mm projector much easier to use. The self-threading and slot-threading projectors have eliminated many of the steps required to place the film in the proper relationship to the sprockets which move the film through the projector, film gate and sound drum, as in a manually threaded projector. Despite the arrival of the easy-to-thread projectors, the manual-threaded projector continues to be offered.

A manually threaded projector, in the opinion of many audiovisual librarians, is still the best machine for projecting a program without danger of damage to the film. A competent projectionist who is in full control of the placement of the film in the critical areas of the film path is the best insurance against expensive film damage. Often, the film being projected matches or exceeds the price of the movie projector itself. An incorrectly threaded projector can result in an expensive repair bill for replacing the torn film.

The Bell and Howell model, 1579, priced at $798.00; Eastman Kodak Company model, Pageant Sound AV-126-TR, at $925.00; Eiki International Incorporated model, RM-O, at $807.00; Elmo Manufacturing Company model, F16-250HS, at $1250.00; Kalart Victor Corporation model, 70-15, at

$717. 00; Kalart Victor model, 80-25, at $952. 00; Singer Education Systems model, 1015, at $806. 00; and Viewlex Audio Visual model, M43E, at $860. 00, can be used for public library film programs. The main differences between these projectors are the built-in speaker versus the detachable speaker located in the projector's cover, audio power output, and the type of projection lamp (tungsten halogen lamp or incandescent bulb). Detachable speakers are preferred for their fidelity in sound reproduction and the ability to disperse sound to a large audience. A built-in speaker eliminates the several steps required to connect and locate the external speaker before and after a film showing. As with audio hardware, the wattage of the amplifier indicates the ability of the projector's sound system to fill the viewing area with audio. Incandescent projection bulbs which operate under the same principle as the standard light bulb are less efficient in producing light output (lumens) than tungsten halogen lamps utilizing a special filament.

The Kodak AV126-TR, Kalart Victor 70-15, Kalart Victor 70-25, and the Singer 1015 utilize the incandescent projector lamp. In view of the rising electrical rates, the power consumption required by these bulbs might be considered a disadvantage. Incandescent lamps also tend to emit less light output.

The Bell and Howell 1579, Eiki RM-O and the Viewlex M43E projectors have tungsten halogen bulbs and built-in speakers. External speakers are available as an accessory, adding between $75. 00 and $150. 00 to the purchase price of the projector. The Eiki seems to have better optics, and project a sharper image. The Eiki, when operating, however, is very noisy, and the location of replacement parts for the Eiki may be more difficult than for the Bell and Howell or Viewlex models.

The two manually threaded projectors offering both tungsten halogen projection lamps and external speakers are the Elmo F16-250HS and the Kalart Victor 80-25. These two projectors are designed to provide many years of reliable service. The Elmo unit is completely free of the so-called "lifetime" self-lubricated parts which rarely perform after 1000 hours of operation. A continuous oil bath of the key parts significantly reduces wear on the excellently tooled mechanical parts of the Elmo unit.

While the Kalart Victor does not have continuous lubrication, it is also known for its reliability. The Kalart Victor projector product line offers a unique film damage detection system which disengages the drive mechanism in the event that a cause of damage exists. The Kalart Victor manual projector is extremely difficult to thread. Despite the complex threading of the Kalart Victor's 80-25 and the Elmo F16-250HS expensive price tag, these units disprove the current trite saying, "They don't build them the way they used to. "

Self-threading projectors were designed to simplify the threading of a motion picture projector. The operator of a self-threader is only required to trim the end of the film with a special cutter and then insert the end into the designated point in the projector. The film is then pushed by sprockets along a track through the projector and out near the take-up reeL. The AIC Photo Incorporated model, Bauer P6, at $1150. 00; Bell and Howell model, 1585A, at $849. 00; Eiki RT-O, at $897. 00; Elmo 16AS, at $1790. 00; Viewlex M43TE, at $885. 00; and Viewlex M16TA-System 16, at $899. 99, will satisfy most small public library applications. All of these projectors except the Elmo have built-in speakers. The Bell and Howell 1585A and Viewlex

M43TE have lower audio output power than the other projectors. Nonetheless, all of the units will meet large group
needs if an extension speaker is used. These projectors
have tungsten halogen bulbs.

The main setback to self-threading projectors is the
handling of the film itself. Despite the care that the manufacturers have taken in the design of the hardware, the possibility always exists that the flexible film stock will fail to
navigate all the turns or engage properly with the sprockets.
For these reasons, a large number of film librarians are
hesitant to recommend self-threading projectors.

Self-threaders can safely handle film if the projectionist takes the necessary step of preparing the film prior
to inserting it into the unit and frequently inspects the condition of the sprocket holes on the film as it leaves the
projector. Regardless of the kind of projector used, a con-
sciencious projectionist is the best insurance against film
damage. Unfortunately, competent projectionists are few in
number and the self-threading projector, being so easy to
use, instills a false confidence in the operator who lacks
the knowledge of proper techniques to prevent film damage.

Bell and Howell has sold more self-threading projectors than its competitors. As a result of the wide ac-
ceptance of the Bell and Howell Autoload, service on the
unit is readily available whether or not the servicing agent
is a Bell and Howell dealer.

Elmo F16-250HS is an example of excellent tooling
and careful design. Unfortunately, the number of dealers
offering the Elmo product line is limited. The Bauer P6
also is offered by a relatively small number of audiovisual
dealers. Viewlex has a larger number of vendors selling
its product line. The Viewlex M16TA requires more steps

to perform prior to projection than the other self-threaders.
The Viewlex M43TE, however, is as easy to operate as the
other self-threading units. The Eiki RT-O is also very easy
to use and has been well constructed. As with the manual
version of this model, the RT-O is very noisy.

Sensitive to film librarians' concern over the potential of film damage by self-threading projectors and the reported difficulty novice projectionists have with manually
threaded projectors, the 16mm projection equipment manufacturers introduced the slot-threading projector. This kind
of unit is extremely easy to use (some claim faster than a
self-threader) and more gentle on the film itself. Unlike
self-threaders, slot-loading projectors permit easy removal
of the film at any point during its showing, in the event that
a problem arises or if one simply wants to quit. Many of
the slot loaders allow the rewinding of the film without removing it from the film track inside the projector itself.

Slot-threading projectors are basically manual. The
operator pulls the film along a slot in the front of the unit.
By performing this task, the film is then placed in the proper location relative to the sprockets, film gate, and sound
drum. By the turn of a knob or the lifting of a lever, depending on the model, all the sprocket covers, the film
shoe, and the tension rollers around the sound drum are
moved into place and then locked in position.

The Bell and Howell model, 1580A, at $829.00; Elmo
model, 16-CL, at $789.00; Kalart Victor model, 90-25, at
$850.00; and the Singer model, 2110, at $865.00, can meet
the needs of public libraries. The Bell and Howell 1580A
is the only slot-threaded projector which does not allow the
rewinding of the film in track; as a result the operator is
forced to remove the film from the projector. The 1580A

does offer a sharp focus picture and good sound reproduction.
The Elmo 76-CL does not offer continuous lubrication as is
found on other models in the Elmo product line. The Elmo
does perform well. It does lack a hard front cover and as
a result might not withstand the wear placed on it if the library decided to circulate projectors to the patron for home
use. The Kalart Victor 90-25 offers the film safety switch
system which gives added protection against film damage.
The 90-25 comes with the most powerful sound amplifier of
all the slot loaders. The Singer 2110 is the new version of
the Singer 1115A. The Singer Education Systems have a
distinct advantage over all competitors offering slot-threading units. Singer introduced the slot-threading projector
and has sold the most units. As a result, from four years
of field experience, the Singer 1115 has been debugged and
the improvements are now found on its successor, the 2110.
The Kalart Victor 90-25 was the second unit brought on the
market and should prove to be a good alternate choice to
the Singer.

8mm Motion Picture Projectors

The use of 8mm by the consumer market continues
to grow. The 8mm format has undergone changes in the
past several years. A newer version of 8mm film called
"Super-8" has a larger frame and the resulting projected
image has better definition. The addition of a sound track
has made Super-8 film an attractive format.

Libraries beginning 8mm collections or maintaining
present collections are faced with the problem that there
still are many regular 8mm film projectors in use. A
regular 8 (standard-8) is unable to project Super-8 film.
Today, projection hardware manufacturers offer, in addition

to models only able to accept Super-8 film, projectors which can handle both regular 8 and Super-8 film. These units are referred to as "dual-8." Public libraries require the flexibility of the dual-8 models.

The use of Super-8 in cartridges is limited for the most part to educational and industrial applications. The consumer market's format is the open reel which requires the projectionist to perform more steps prior to projection than are necessary with the Technicolor or Fairchild continuous loop cartridge. Most public library patrons own open reel projectors.

Silent Super-8 or dual-8 open reel projectors are manufactured exclusively for the consumer market. There are many models and brand names available and the problem facing the library is the availability of local service. Name brands such as Argus, Bell and Howell, GAF, Kodak, Sears and Wards are preferred.

The second problem facing the library is reliability. The designers of the 8mm projector never intended it to be used in a public library by the general public. Therefore, there is no dependable silent dual-8 projector available for library use. Several libraries have reported relative success with the Bell and Howell dual-8 model, 1620A projector, priced at $149.95. Whatever brand and model the public library purchases, it should be a very basic unit without any extra features such as a variable speed control or a zoom lens.

Super-8 sound projectors are being manufactured to meet the heavy use experienced in the educational/industrial markets. All but one model allow the recording or rerecording of the sound track to accompany the visual presentation. This feature is desirable if the public library wishes to

produce its own films. The Eumig (U. S. A.) Incorporated
model, S807D, at $428.00, and the Karl Heitz Incorporated
model, Norimat SD, priced at $369.50, offer the flexibility
of projecting silent regular 8 and Super-8 as well as sound
Super-8. The Bell and Howell model, 1742A, at $324.95;
Elmo model, ST800, at $399.95; Eumig model S802, at
$353.00; and Karl Heitz model, Norimat S, at $339.50,
should meet most library's recording requirements. All of
these units are similar in their quality of performance. In
view of the large network of service locations, the Bell and
Howell is preferred.

The Bell and Howell model 1733A is a playback-only
sound Super-8 projector. No other manufacturer offers a
straight playback unit. The 1733A sells for $249.95.

There are many Super-8 projectors with built-in
screens which allow the viewing of film in lighted areas in
the library. Most utilize a cartridge and therefore are in-
compatible to an open reel projector format. The Kodak
model, Supermatic 60, at $545.00; Elmo model, SC-8T, at
$799.00; and the Eumig model, AV3000, at $370.00, permit the viewing of open reel film with a built-in screen as
well as front projection onto a wall-hung or tripod screen.
The Kodak Supermatic 60 requires the operator to place the
open reel film inside a cassette which is then inserted into
the projector. The Kodak model and the Elmo SC-8T are
sound projectors, while the Eumig AV3000 is a silent unit.
From a service aspect, the Kodak unit is preferred.

The Fairchild Camera and Instrument Corporation
model, Cart-Reel 31, at $489.00, offers sound Super-8 play-
back only on a built-in screen. Open reel film must be
placed into a specially designed cartridge before playback
on these projectors.

Filmstrip Projectors

Filmstrips have been in use by schools for many years. Their popularity has grown as the result of the addition of sound. The filmstrip, in conjunction with an audio cassette or record, can offer a program with a visual presentation synchronized with a sound track.

Front projection filmstrip units come as manual (hand-operated); semi-automatic, in which a motorized assembly advances the film to the next frame at the command of the operator pushing a button; and automatic projectors, which are coupled to a cassette player or phonograph record player which reacts to pre-recorded signals to advance to the next frame.

Manually operated filmstrip projectors are offered by a large number of manufacturers. These units operate very similarly. Many of the units offer the ability to project 35-mm slides. The main difference between models in a particular product line is in ability to produce a bright image on the screen. The wattage rating of the projection lamps usually indicates the ability of the bulb to generate high light output. Projection units with a 500- to 700-watt bulb rating are brighter than those units employing 50- to 150-watt lamps.

Projection units utilizing bulbs with a rating of 150 watts or less should be excluded from consideration when a library is selecting a filmstrip projector. The brightness of the image produced will prove unsatisfactory in situations where the distance between the projector and the screen is great and the room can not be completely darkened.

Projectors using lamps with a rating of 300 watts can perform well in most situations. A/V Concepts Corporation model, SFS-300N, at $84.00; Bell and Howell model, 746B, at $144.95; DuKane Corporation model, 28A33,

at $85. 00; Singer model, SM-44, at $75. 00; Standard Projection and Equipment Company model, 666CN, at $87. 50;
and Viewlex model, V-25 Lumenmaster, at $116. 95, can
meet public library needs if the room in which they are to
be used can be fairly well darkened.

If lighting is a problem or the distance between the
projector and the screen is great, the DuKane model, 28A75,
at $135. 00; Singer model, School Master 750, at $152. 00;
Standard Projector model, 750 RR-2, at $160. 00; and View-
lex model, V-25 Lumenmaster with a 750-watt CWA bulb, at
$136. 95, will work well.

Semi-automatic units which allow remote operation
are the Bell and Howell model, 747BL (300 watts), priced
at $194. 95; DuKane model 28A56 (500 watts), at $160. 00;
Singer model, SM-400RC (300 watts), at $143. 00; Singer
model SM-1000RC (500 watts), at $198. 00; Singer model,
School Master 500 Remote (500 watts), at $173. 00; Singer
model, School Master 750 Remote (750 watts), at $194. 00;
and the Viewlex model, V-25R Lumenmaster (300 watts), at
$165. 95.   By connecting any one of these projectors to a
cassette player with a built-in synchronizer which is able to
sense a 50 Hertz superimposed signal, pre-recorded sound
filmstrip programs from publishers can be presented to
large audiences.

Automatic sound filmstrip projectors combine a semi-
automatic projector with a cassette player or record player
with a built-in synchronizer.   The DuKane model, 28A15C
Cassette Super Micromatic, at $365. 00; McClure Projectors
Incorporated model, MRF-3, at $179. 00; Singer model, In-
structor, at $379. 50; Standard Projector model, CR300-1
Cartridge Load, at $225. 00; and Viewlex model, Viewtalk
Cassette Series VHCR 2551-Automatic, at $389. 95, are

playback-only units. The Standard Projector CP 300-1 requires the placement of the filmstrip into a cartridge before it can be fed into the projector mechanism. The Singer Instructor and the Viewlex VHCR 2551 employ 500-watt bulbs and offer more audio output power; thus they are better for large audience showings.

The Standard Projector model, 1001RP, at $440.00, permits the recording and pulsing of the sound track, thus allowing more creative uses for silent filmstrips.

The sound filmstrip utilizing a phonograph record is rapidly being replaced in popularity by the audio cassette. Libraries beginning audiovisual filmstrip service would be wise to exclude this format from their new collections.

Individual viewing of silent filmstrips is possible through use of a silent filmstrip projector with a built-in screen. The Beacon model, FS-150, at $39.95, with a 24-square-inch screen; Hudson Photographic Industries Incorporated model, Prima HPI 331-2, at $33.00, with a 20-square-inch screen; and the Singer model, Study-Mate II, at $31.50, with a 12-inch square screen, are extremely portable. The Viewlex model, Superviewer V134, at $83.95, with a 35-square-inch screen, is preferable for use within the library.

Sound filmstrip projectors with built-in screens differ primarily in screen size and audio output power. The larger the screen and/or audio output rating is, the more expensive the unit will be. The Bell and Howell model, Knowledge Master 762A, at $310.00; Charles Beseler Company model, 3551, at $199.95; DuKane model, 28A1, at $310.00; Singer model, Auto-Vance II Study-Mate, at $149.50; Singer model, Insta 35 8120, at $350.00; Standard Projector model LP-10-2, at $175.00; and the Viewlex model, Superviewer V135, at $234.95, are automatic units which do not have a cartridge system to hold either the filmstrip or the filmstrip and cassette together. The Singer 8120 offers the option of using a cartridge. Except for the Singer Auto-Vance II and the Standard Projector LP-10-2, the sound filmstrip projectors with built-in screens are quite bulky, restricting them to inhouse use in the library. The Singer model, Insta 35, at $435. 00, and the Standard Projector model LP-10-3, at $200. 00, allow the recording of a sound track as well as the pulsing of the tape to control the advance of the filmstrip. The $435. 00 Insta 35 also permits the front projection of filmstrips and as a result can meet most of the small library's filmstrip viewing needs.

Slide Projectors

35mm slides offer greater flexibility in programming than filmstrips which do not permit the rearrangement of frames containing unique visuals. Coupled with a cassette recorder having a built-in synchronizer, the slide projector has become a tool for creative production of audiovisual programs.

Eastman Kodak dominates the slide projector market, both in the consumer market with its Carousel product line and in the educational/industrial market with its Ektagraphic product line. For public library use, the Ektagraphic slide projectors offer a wide assortment of features which can meet the needs of the general use by the public and the requirements of sophisticated presentations. The Kodak Ektagraphic Model E, at $154. 50, due to its simplicity of design, is recommended for the patron use. The Kodak Ektagraphic model, AF-2, is for public libraries planning to utilize slide presentations to audiences requiring professional quality pro-

jection. The AF-2, at $279. 50, provides automatic chang-
ing of slides at a selected interval ranging from five to 15
seconds. This feature is convenient when repetitive showings of a silent slide program are desirable.

Whichever projector is selected, if the library plans
to use the unit at the same distance from the screen as its
16mm motion picture projector, a 7-inch focal length lens
in the slide projector will give the same size image as the
16mm film projector equiped with a 2-inch lens. A filmstrip adaptor for the slide projector will eliminate the need
for a silent filmstrip front projection unit. Filmstrip projectors do allow the use of slides but are limited to the physical insertion of one slide at a time. This proves to be bur-
densome.

Sound slide projectors with a built-in screen allow
the individual to view a tape/slide program in a lighted area
in the library. The Bell and Howell model, Ringmaster 796,
at $389. 50, and the Singer model, Caramate, at $329. 50,
accept the Kodak Carousel slide projector tray and present
a synchronized program to the material recorded on an audio
cassette. The Bell and Howell 796 and the recording version 797 permit front projection for larger audience viewing.
The Singer model, Caramate Record, at $384. 50, like the
Bell and Howell 797, permit the recording of a sound track
as well as the pulse required to change the slide.

Overhead Projectors

The ability to project prepared transparencies and information written on 8-inch by 10-inch clear sheets of film
in lighted rooms is made possible by an overhead projector.
Libraries with meeting room facilities will find the overhead
projector a good alternative to the old-fashioned blackboard.

There is very little difference among brand names or the models within a company's product line. Many of the accessories or special features will never be used--with one exception, the roll attachment. This accessory allows the operator to roll up a clean section of transparent film, thus eliminating the need to erase the written information before proceeding to the next written set of information. The roll attachment with film adds about $25.00 to the purchase price of an overhead unit.

The American Optical Corporation model, 3654 Economy Apollo 6, at $199.00; Bell and Howell model, 36OGCA, at $245.00; Charles Besler model, Porta-Scribe 15710LC, at $182.70; Buhl Projector Company model, 80/14, at $160.00; Elmo model, HP-260, at $349.00; Projection Optics Company model, Transpaque 20/20 21400, at $189.95; and 3M Company model, 213 AKD, at $356.00, offer good performance. Libraries would be very prudent to put a ceiling of $200.00 on the purchase price of an overhead projector.

Opaque Projectors

In recent years, the opaque projector has been overlooked. Unlike the overhead projector, an opaque projector will accept any form of hard copy, such as a printed sheet of paper or a page in a book. To project the same type of material on an overhead projector, the opaque material must be duplicated on transparent film.

The American Optical Corporation model, 3525 High Speed Opaque, priced at $568.00; Beseler model, Vu-Lyte II 6200, at $381.75; Buhl model, Mark IV-009, at $474.00; Projection Optics model, Opascope 20005, at $463.00; and Squibb-Taylor Incorporated model, Taylor Spotlight TS-7, at $482.00, are able to meet public library requirements. All

of these units accept bound books. The Taylor TS-7 seems
to have a very good frequency-of-repair record. Whatever
model is purchased, a dark viewing will be required.

Projection Screens

Front projection screens are designed to meet a variety of lighting conditions existing in the room in which they
are to be used. A glass beaded screen surface is recommended when the library is unable to darken the viewing area
sufficiently. The beaded screen is very efficient in reflect-
ing the projected image back to the audience. To accomplish
this, the reflected light is contained in a very narrow viewing area which requires the audience to sit almost directly
in front of the screen. The image reproduced by the beaded
screen is less defined than with the other types of screen
surfaces. A silver lenticular surface is almost as efficient
as the beaded screen. The silver surface adds "warmth"
to the colors which are reflected back and most people find
this affect pleasing. The lenticular screen allows a larger
viewing area than the beaded screen. The matted screen offers
the widest viewing area while reproducing the least distorted
image. The matted screen, though, requires a dark room.

The quality of screen surfaces offered by the various
manufacturers is basically uniform. Where the difference
lies among various models in a manufacturer's product line
is in the durability of the roller mechanism and the strength
of the tripod. The Da-Lite Screen Company model, Video
A, or Knox Manufacturing Company model, Series 300, are
excellent free-standing (tripod) screens. The Da-Lite model,
Video B; Draper Shade and Screen Company model, Luma;
and Knox model, Series 200, are very good wall-mounted
or ceiling-hung screens.

There is a wide variety of rear projection screens
which allow viewing in a lighted room.   Table-top cabinet-
type projection screens enable the use of front projection
equipment such as a slide projector to be used in a carrel
or on a table.   It is very possible that in order to use the
table-top rear projection screen, a special lens will be required on your projection equipment.

The Advance Products Company Incorporated model,
AV-463, at $229. 95, or the H. Wilson Corporation model,
Movie Mover RP I, at $239. 00, offer a rear screen cabinet
on a mobile projection cart.   Thus any area in the library
can become a viewing station.

Headsets

The headsets purchased for public library patron use
should be manufactured for industrial/educational applications.   These headsets employ stronger wiring in order to
withstand the tugging and pulling that is not normally experienced in a home setting.

The quality of reproduction of all industrial grade
headsets is for the most part the same.   What causes the
difference in prices is the degree of comfort.   The more
padding there is, the more expensive the unit will be.   Librarians selecting headsets should wear for 15 minutes the
models under consideration for purchase.

Videotape Recorders and Players

The use of videotape in the public library is a fairly
recent phenomenon.   Interest in the format was stimulated
with the development of the 3/4-inch cassette, which has
greatly simplified the use of videotape.

For pre-recorded videotape playback, a library will need a video cassette deck playback unit connected to a color television receiver/monitor. The JVC Industries Incorporated model, CP-5000, at $1100. 00; Panasonic Video Systems model, NV-2110M, at $1350. 00; and Sony model, VP-2000, at $1345. 00, are able to play back 3/4-inch videotape cassettes. The Sony VP-2000 has the best frequency-of-repair record of these units and is the most widely used in public libraries.

These playback units may be connected to any television set to reproduce recorded material. Consumer television sets without a receptacle for headsets will have to be modified if the library plans to have individual patrons view video programs. Sony manufactures the best color television sets with screen sizes of 17 inches or smaller. For color sets larger than 17 inches, GTE Sylvania, Magnavox Company, Quasar Electronics Corporation, RCA Consumer Electronics, Sony, and Zenith offer about the same quality color reproduction.

For those libraries planning to record copyright-cleared material from television broadcasts, a video receiver/monitor will be required. This type of television set differs from the consumer set in that it has the necessary modifications to receive a signal and convert it to the proper configuration to enable the video recorder to store the program. Receiver/monitors are available from most manufacturers of videotape hardware.

Those libraries desiring to video-record events or library programs, and to produce information programs will require the flexibility of a portable unit. JVC model, CR-4400U portable, at $2695. 00, and Sony model, VO-3800, at $3000. 00, offer on-location color videotape recording on 3/4-inch cassette. Thus, the portable recorder will pro-

duce the same cartridge format as the in-house playback
unit requires. The Sony recorder is preferred.
To accompany the video recorder, a monochrome
(black and white) camera will meet basic library needs. The
hand-held JVC model, GS-4600, at $695.00, for use with the
JVC recorder, or the Sony portable camera model, AVC-
3450, at $750.00, for use with the Sony recorder, will satis-
fy on-location recording. If the library prefers a camera
for use on a tripod, the Hitachi Shibaden Corporation of
America model, FP-71, at $595.00, or the Sony model, AVC-
3250, at $500.00, should be considered. Either camera will
work with the tape recorders listed. Unlike the hand held
cameras, the Hitachi FP-71 and Sony AVC-3250 do not have
built-in microphones. Electro Voice, Shure, and Sony are
manufacturers of a wide variety of microphones. The Sony
model, ECM-16, at $37.00, is a good lapel microphone.
This type of microphone eliminates the recording problem
which arises when the person speaking moves away from or
too close to the microphone. The Shure model, 516 EQ, at
$70.00, is a table or hand-held microphone with built-in
filters to compensate for a variety of acoustical problems
which one might face.

As the library gains proficiency in creative video production, purchases such as a color camera, an editor, a
film chain and/or multiplexer will become attractive. The
availability of local television production facilities in neighborhood schools and academic institutions or industrial organizations might relieve the public library from establishing its own facility.

With the introduction of home video recorders by
Sony and Quasar, as well as the pending arrival of the
video disc, the public library is on the threshold of a new

media boom.   But regardless of the format, the sign of a
good piece of audiovisual hardware will always be that the
unit does not draw attention to itself when reproducing library material.   It is the information or enjoyment stored
in audiovisual software that is important, and no matter how
impressive or good the playback equipment is, it can not
improve what has already been captured on film or magnetic
tape.   A good piece of audiovisual equipment will only make
the non-book experience trouble free.

Notes

1. National Audio-Visual Association, Inc.   The Audio-Visual
    Equipment Directory, edited by Sally Hericks (Fairfax,
    Virginia: National Audio-Visual Association, 1976-77).

2. The MP Audio PT 95 is designed for use with headsets
    only.   Up to four pairs of earphones may be used at any
    time with this unit.

Chapter 3

SERVICES

William Sloan

Services are the culmination of all the planning, collection building, catalog preparation, and personnel training that go into establishing an audiovisual center. Indeed, it is services that define the role of the public library. And what is that role? Essentially it is to serve as an educational institution that provides for the informal educational needs of the community. In this it is unique. Schools and colleges, although they sometimes overlap the services of public libraries, are institutions that provide formal education. Recently, these lines of differentiation among educational institutions have grown less clear, especially with the growth in colleges of independent study and the "school-without-walls" concept, and--a parallel movement--the development in public libraries of "independent learner" projects. At the same time, inter-institution cooperation is growing, as is the concept of library networks. Thus, it may well be that in the next decade we may have to re-define the roles of schools, colleges, and public libraries. However, the traditional pattern of service still prevails generally in public libraries: they remain institutions that support informal learning. It is with this role in mind that I will be discussing audiovisual services.

58

Circulation

Of all the services in an AV center, circulation is probably the most important. However, the circulation of nonprint materials, and especially films, presents certain special problems that are unique to nonprint and that must be dealt with effectively if the service itself is to be effective. Of all the various media the one most sought after by the public is films. Yet, rarely does the borrower see the film ahead of time, even where a previewing service is offered. This is not the case with a book, which the reader will usually have browsed through before borrowing it. He or she takes the film on trust: first, by trusting that the films have been intelligently selected by specialists; secondly, by relying on the guidance of the catalog description; and thirdly, by accepting advice provided in person by the staff. Since the people actually issuing the film, or taking the booking in the first place, are clericals who have rarely seen the film, they usually are not in a position to give advice. They are, however, usually the people first asked for advice by the public. They have to be carefully trained and tactfully guided by the librarians, so that they will turn over advisory questions to the professionals. The smooth integration of clerical and professional responsibilities is essential for an effective circulation service.

Who Do Public Libraries Serve?

Ideally, films and other nonprint media should be available to everyone in the community, with no holds barred. In practice, the philosophy of the public library as an institution of informal education is applied in a restrictive sense in the vast majority of American public libraries. Thus,

the general rule is that films may not be borrowed for classroom use.   This is, in fact, a practical rule, for the demand
by schools for films is so insatiable that were borrowing
privileges opened to them, there would be few films left for
the community at large--groups such as nursing homes, community centers, religious groups, hospitals, prisons, etc.
and individuals that make up the bulk of library film users.

Also, in many libraries, nonprint collections have been set
up with federal funding and are restricted by the legislation
from allowing schools to borrow films.   However, restrictions on school use can make for bad public relations, especially in a smaller community.   It seems likely, in the
future, that libraries will find ways of being less restrictive
so that enrichment of films can find their way into the classroom, perhaps on some limited basis.   But while school use
is a factor in staff work loads, basically it does not affect
the way in which the circulation functions to serve users:
the object still is to get the right medium to the right user
on the right day.

It is not the purpose of this paper to outline all the
records necessary to operate a circulation system, as this
information is readily available elsewhere.   I would point
out that the key record in a reservation-circulation system
is the calendar form used for each print of a film title that
is to be loaned (or each item of nonprint material that is
to be made available on a reservation system).   The reservation dates are entered on the calendar.   Supporting the
calendar record are various charging/confirmation forms.
Perhaps the best two sources on circulation problems and
systems are George Rehrauer's book, The Film User's
Handbook (R. R. Bowker, 1975) and an audiotape on the
management of circulation that is sold by the Educational

Film Library Association (EFLA, 43 West 61st St., New
York, N. Y. 10023).

One thing to remember in setting up a circulation system is to keep it simple. Because nonprint items, especially
16mm films, are expensive, there is a tendency when initiating a nonprint service to keep overly elaborate records
in order to control loss. However, complicated forms and
too elaborate records will in the long run prove too expensive to maintain. The most practical step to take after one
has done the necessary background reading is to visit two
or three libraries that circulate films. Actually examining
a practical circulation service in operation will help you
identify what is and what is not essential in such an operation.

Reference and Advisory Services

Providing reference and advisory services to the public is entirely the responsibility of the professional librarian.
Next to making purchase decisions for the collection, it is
the most interesting and challenging work in an AV library.
Reference work can range from simple questions such as
"where can I rent Nanook of the North, " to complex requests
such as drawing up a filmography on aging for a group of
people who are within a few years of retirement. The range
of questions in a public library is exceptionally wide, and
they are not just on sources for films, filmstrips, videotapes,
slides, etc., but are also related to equipment, new technology, distribution, film festivals and film history from the
avant-garde to Hollywood features. Limitations on the amount
of service given depend upon the amount of staff time available. Most libraries are prepared to carry out quick searches
in response to queries by phone, in person or by mail.
Twenty years ago, in a quieter age, it was customary for

film reference librarians to compile long filmographies for
patrons. The usual practice today is for the librarian to
show the reader how to use the reference materials, and
expect him or her to do the necessary bibliographic work.
The question of drawing up a program or film series for
an organization is somewhat different. While users should
be encouraged to use the library's catalog, if they have not
seen the films they are going to need the programming help
of a librarian who has.

It is beyond the scope of this article to list all the
media reference materials--books, periodicals, pamphlets--
necessary to maintain a reference/advisory service. I will
list a few important ones, and some organizations and services to which the library should subscribe. First there is
the "family" of media and multimedia indexes issued by the
National Information Center for Educational Media, known
as the NICEM indexes. A complete listing of the titles available can be obtained from NICEM, University of Southern
California, University Park, Los Angeles, California 90007.
Every AV library should have NICEM's Index to 16mm Educational Films and its Index to 35mm Filmstrips. However,
I have found that the public rarely makes use of the other
volumes in the series, and those libraries with small book
budgets find sources for other media than films and filmstrips through other reference books and pamphlets. The
NICEM indexes are oriented to the school user and are often
not as helpful with the general public as one would wish.
Because of inherent weaknesses in the NICEM indexes it is
also necessary to acquire the reference work, Films and
Other Materials for Projection, issued in book form by the
Library of Congress. LC's specific approach to subject
headings makes it relatively easy to use these volumes. Also,

they conveniently list most nonprint media, with the exception of videotape, together in one alphabet.

Another common question in libraries is for sources of feature films that are in nontheatrical release. James Limbacher's Feature Films on 8 and 16, published by Bowker and reissued approximately every three years, is essential for answering this type of question. It lists mostly 16mm films, with a few 8mm titles. Between issues of the book, supplements come out in the centerfold of Sightlines magazine.

The above reference books are a beginning. For additional titles there are listings and evaluations of media reference books in the following issues of Film Library Quarterly (copies may be ordered from Box 348, Radio City Station, New York, N. Y. 10019):

> "The Film Library's Book Collection, Basic Reference Books, " by Naomi Weiss, Volume 3, No. 3, 1970;

> "More Basic Reference Books, " by Nadine Covert, Volume 5, No. 4, 1972;

> "Information Sources, " by Barbara Humphreys and Julie Semkow, Volume 7, No. 3&4 (combined issue), 1974;

> "Film Books for Students and Teachers, " by Nancy Manley, Volume 9, No. 2, 1976.

Bibliographic control for films and media is more chaotic than it is for books. Moreover, there is the additional problem of getting good evaluations of the material. For that reason it is necessary to build a pamphlet file arranged by subject to support the reference book collection. Key items in the pamphlet files are the specialized bibliographies issued by library, media, film, and other organiza-

tions. How does one find out about these bibliographies?
By taking out memberships in professional organizations and
getting their periodicals; for example, the American Library
Association's Booklist, the Educational Film Library Associ-
ation's Sightlines, and the Film Library Information Council's
Film Library Quarterly.

    There are also other periodicals which are valuable
for listings of new films and videotapes, and for specialized
subject bibliographies. For film these include: Film News,
Film and Broadcasting Review, Landers Film Reviews, and
Previews. For video there are Videography and CVRP Patch
Panel.

Outreach

    Traditionally, advisory service in the audiovisual area
has been strictly in-house. In recent years, however, a few
public libraries have had media specialists go out into the
community to work with groups and organizations. Some of
the first instances of media specialists carrying out this kind
of activity occurred during the poverty programs under the
Kennedy Administration. This practice received further im-
petus at the beginning of the half-inch video movement in
the late sixties and early seventies. However, with the
tightening of library budgets in the mid-seventies it seems
to be a declining service. Nevertheless, it is a worthy goal
of any public library to have a film or video specialist take
films and videotapes to groups that rarely or perhaps never
use the library, and open up via the media a whole world
of ideas and information. It seems a particularly appropriate activity at this time because there is a wealth of
fascinating material coming out of the independent film and
video movement that is creating works rarely seen by most

people. These include works from major documentary film-
makers and from obscure video groups working in communes.
This type of outreach--meeting the needs of people who do
not come to the library--is a service that libraries have
barely begun to tap.

The Study Center Concept

Perhaps the newest service in public library audiovisual departments is the Media Study Center. To some degree public libraries have long served as places where the
public could come and study film, video and other nonprint
media. Nevertheless, the study center concept is new in
that it takes these past services, formalizes them, and provides an in-depth service. It borrows the concept from
study centers for film that have been provided by the Library of Congress, the Museum of Modern Art, and graduate
cinema programs in larger universities. The idea is also
drawn from the Independent Learner project in libraries.
The philosophy behind it is that media are worth studying
intently and carefully, more carefully than a once-through
projection.

A Study Center in a public library is different from
those in the institutions where the idea began. There, it
has been a facility for the graduate student of media under
the tutelage of a professor. In a public library the situation
is often just the opposite. The user often is not a specialist
in the medium under study. He or she is often not familiar
with film history, genres, styles, video art movements.
Indeed, the public library patron's interest may be more in
the information contained in the medium than in studying
media itself. It is the media specialist-librarian manning
the Study Center who provides the user with guidance to

the material. In effect the media specialist becomes the
mentor. The initial interview is extremely important. The
media specialist must ascertain the educational level of the
user, what his or her goals are, how deeply the user should
get into the material, and which medium would be best for
the user's purpose.

Study centers are costly. They require skilled staff.
They require expensive equipment: analytical and flatbed
viewers for film, a variety of tape decks for video to handle
the different formats, and 8mm and 16mm film projectors,
slide viewers, and filmstrip viewers. But one can start
with conventional projectors and the simplest of video cassette players. Media study is mushrooming in colleges and
universities. As a result, student interns will often work
in media study centers for no pay, in return for experience
and course credits. In many libraries the video equipment
is available, having been acquired through various specially
funded projects. The Study Center is still at the innovative
stage and because it is new, grant monies can often be acquired to get the operation started. In time the library administration may see it as a basic service and give it basic
support. There is a lively, bright, educated, and growing
group of young people who are turned on to getting their information through media. They are the future users of the
Media Study Center. It is a service worth fighting for in
public libraries.

Chapter 4

SPACE AND FACILITIES

Patricia del Mar

Traditionally, libraries beginning audiovisual services have been more concerned with the "what" and the "who" than with the "where." Provision of recordings and films from makeshift quarters by staff with art and music backgrounds has often been the pattern. In the 1930s and 1940s library directors assumed that circulation came before adequate space and facilities. How else to convince trustees or city/county officials of the need for such "esoteric" services? The patron was satisfied with film showings in so-called multi-purpose rooms (usually unsuitable for any one purpose), or with listening to recordings in telephone booth-like rooms, and marveled at the ingenuity and cheerfulness of the library staff.

Small public libraries now building or remodeling existing structures can benefit by all the trial-and-error experiences accumulated over the years. There is a growing awareness of what Don Roberts calls "technocensorship."[1] Roberts means not just the obvious censorship involved in not purchasing non-print media, but that imposed by having projection facilities which offer unacceptable screen reproduction, and audio facilities equally below standard. We must begin to consider the integrity of the media and not

be satisfied with less than our best delivery system. Library directors, at this point, should not throw up their
hands and their building remodeling plans and say if we cannot afford everything, we had better do nothing. On the con-
trary, one should look at non-print space and facilities as a
long-term project and an investment in the future. The
phenomenal growth of non-print in the past 30 years will be
accelerated in the future by cable TV and videodiscs. Careful planning now will make future budgeting easier.

Published guidelines, standards, or even information
on space planning for audiovisual service is scarce. Librarians have been preoccupied with selection, circulation
and programming of audiovisual materials, and this pre-
occupation is mirrored in the library literature. Research
has been concerned with the number and kinds of titles which
should be provided per patron. In 1975 the Audiovisual Committee of the Public Library Association of the American
Library Association published Recommendations for Audiovisual Materials and Services for Small and Medium-sized
Public Libraries. [2] The chairperson of that committee is
the editor of this book. While the committee recognized
that quantitative standards are no longer adequate or acceptable, a start had to be made. Until valid research can
prove or disprove the correctness of educated guesses, at
least a dialogue can now begin. Less than two pages of
the ALA publication were devoted to space and equipment
(as compared with two chapters in this book). Even those
two short pages, though, may be enough to scare off the
neophyte with their "musts" and their "shoulds. " This
author is aware of many public libraries which would be
overjoyed to have the luxury of even such minimum standards.
       The other major published work on space design is the

two-part article by William J. Speed, "An Ideal Film Library," published ten years ago in the Film Library Quarterly.[3] Speed based his conclusions on 17 years of experience as director of the Audio-Visual Department at the Los Angeles Public Library. He was also unofficial consultant to many a perplexed AV librarian, as I can attest from 12 years of professional association. The second part of his article deals with libraries serving 50,000-100,000 population, because the author feels that a minimum population of 50,000 is needed to support a film collection.

Both the ALA and FLIC publications should be thoroughly studied, but today's library director may well not be designing for a conventional independent public library serving 100,000 and with minimal access to other libraries. The possible variations are many:

1. Main library or branch library?

2. If a branch, full-service, storefront or neighborhood center?

3. Fixed location or mobile?

4. Completely independent or part of some system, network, cooperative or circuit?

5. Located in a state in which AV materials are circulated by the state library?

6. Isolated geographically or within easy driving distance of larger public libraries with reciprocal borrowing agreements?

Those are but the most obvious initial determinations to be made. In addition, the director must attempt to plan for ten to 25 years hence, when public libraries as we know them may be unrecognizable.

To complicate matters further, there is a growing movement in librarianship which questions the very separate-

ness of audiovisual service or materials and argues for total
(or almost total) integration of print and non-print. The
design of the library can help or hinder such integration.
Let's assume that you have thought out all these philo-
sophical problems and have drawn up a building statement.
Whether audiovisual will be a distinct department or integrated
with print departments, an irreducible minimum of space and
equipment is required.

1. Public Service Area

     This area includes shelving for reference books, peri-
odicals, film and record catalogs, self-use materials such
as recordings, 8mm films, loops, filmstrip sets and any
equipment for in-house use. Non-browsable materials, 16mm
films and audio cassettes, will be stored behind the check-
out or reference desk. Tables and chairs and lounge furniture enable the borrower to study the printed material and
individually preview some formats. Since the number of
patrons using the collection varies throughout the day, flexible space which is shared with another department might be
preferable to a totally enclosed space. If audiovisual is to
be open the same hours as the rest of the library this should
not present any problems. Shelving for recordings should
be a combination of free-standing low browsing bins and conventional metal or wooden recording shelving. In purchasing
shelving emphasis should be on movable partitions or shelves.
There is little uniformity in media packaging and one can
only assume that future purchases will require still another
configuration of shelving.

2. Circulation Area

Adjacent to the public service area should be the circulation control or reference desk.   All materials are reserved here, checked out for in-house use or outside loan.
The audiovisual librarian will spend time here assisting patrons with reference queries, program planning, the location
of material not available in the library, etc.   A clerk or
para-professional will ordinarily staff the area; therefore, a
minimum of two work stations is required.   My personal
preference is for an L-shaped countertop height (54 inches)
because of the greater amount of storage space this makes
available.   The area will contain copies of the film catalog,
the card catalog for recordings, and files for reserving material and equipment.   If the department plays recordings
and cassettes for patrons on a master console, this would
also be housed here.   Headphone storage would be required
in any case, as headphones are prone to dispppear if left
unattended on tables or in carrels.

3. Media Storage Area

All 16mm films should be stored on end in metal
film racks adjacent to the control desk.   Any other media
can be stored in this non-public area for security purposes.
The area should be totally enclosed and lockable.   Allow
wide aisles so that film trucks and equipment can pass through
easily.   While media absolutely require a minimum fluctua-
tion of temperature and humidity, this same consideration
should view proper ventilation and humidity control as a
frill.

4. Office for AV Librarian

    A fully-enclosed office, this should include an execu-
tive-type desk and chair, four to eight vertical or lateral
file drawers, six stacks of six-shelf bookcases, three chairs
for staff conferences, salesmen or visitors, a bulletin board,
typewriter and table. The shelving is needed for professional
publications, review sources, LC music and motion picture
catalogs, material awaiting processing, etc.

5. Work Area

    Space is required for at least two desks or work sta-
tions for clerical work. This includes compiling circulation
statistics, typing monthly and annual reports, answering mail
requests, writing for preview prints of films, etc. In addition, a table or counter is needed for packing and mailing
materials and cleaning recordings. Storage for bulky items
such as film shipping cartons, recording jackets, film leader,
film cement, film reels, etc. should probably fill one wall.

    16mm film inspection requires an electronic film in-
spection machine and space for the film inspector to move
trucks loaded with films to be inspected and then shelved.
A small library could begin with hand inspection and a simple table-top motor-driven rewind, but the more expensive
electronic inspection machine will pay for itself in better
quality and longer-lasting films and, therefore, a better
served public.

6. Film Screening Space

    To this point everything listed is commonly found in
small libraries with active audiovisual programs. Space for
the screening of films by staff is very rare. More often

preview films must be screened in an office, a workroom or public meeting room or auditorium. This is unsatisfactory for several reasons. Trying to decide whether to spend $400 for a library film is a serious responsibility and requires the best possible viewing conditions: a room with carefully designed sound and visual qualities. A wall-hung screen, speakers connected to the adjoining projection booth or area in the workroom, chairs with movable writing tablets, dimmer controls for the lighting and blackout shades or drapes to block out light sources complete this room. The public meeting room in any active library is usually only available from midnight to 9 A.M. Returned films which may be damaged should be screened immediately. Without a preview room, this may be difficult. Films tend to pile up to the point where huge blocks of time are needed for screening, and phone calls must be made or follow-up letters sent to patrons who may have returned damaged films.

7. Individualized Listening/Viewing Facilities

One criticism of audiovisual services in the past concerned the emphasis on serving groups to the detriment of individuals. This has not been as true with recordings, although library-sponsored music classes and appreciation groups have received special treatment. With today's commitment to the independent learner, even small public libraries are gearing up to the challenge of individualized audiovisual service. Existing carrels and tables can be modified by the provision of electrical outlets or junction boxes so that listening and viewing are possible throughout the building. Patrons should be able to use the library's own media, and also study on their own through "Open University"-type programs.

8. Production Area

How many libraries, of whatever size, offer production
facilities? Here is a case of history inhibiting the future.
School children learn how to copy photographs or slides, make
transparencies, tape stories and music. Why shouldn't the
public library continue this service for them as adults? Our
print-dominated profession sees photocopy machines for print
as basic, but neglects to provide the capability of reproducing
audiovisual material. Slide copying equipment is available
for less than $200. 00, transparency equipment for less than
$500. 00. A darkroom is not necessary for most production
equipment and space could be found in many public or non-
public areas for both storage and use. The popularity of
library-produced slide/tape programs attests to the ease of
use and availability of inexpensive projectors and tape recorders.

When ordering furniture and equipment you should:

1. Study the literature, especially the titles
    listed at the end of this chapter.

2. Collect dealer catalogs.

3. Confer with colleagues who have recent build-
    ing experience.

4. Talk with exhibitors at ALA, AECT and your
    state library association annual conference.

5. Visit libraries, especially school and commu-
    nity college libraries which have up-to-date
    media programs.

6. Solicit advice from experts in other city de-
    partments, especially electrical and building
    trade employees.

7. Ask for assistance from your state library
    audiovisual consultant, system audiovisual co-
    ordinator or film circuit administrator.

Now that you have considered the possible space allocations for audiovisual services and have tested the suggestions against your building program, you will, it is hoped, be better able to design a service that meets your present needs and future dreams.

Notes

1. Roberts, Don. "Technocensorship," Sightlines 10:3 (Spring 1977), 4.

2. American Library Association. Public Library Association. Audiovisual Committee. Recommendations for Audiovisual Materials and Services for Small and Medium-Sized Public Libraries. Chicago: ALA, 1975.

3. Speed, William J. "An Ideal Film Library," Film Library Quarterly 1:1 (Winter 1967-68), 17-20, and 1:2 (Spring 1968), 23-26.

References

1. National Audio-Visual Association. The Audio-visual Equipment Directory. 23rd ed., 1977-1978. Fairfax, Virginia: NAVA, 1977.

2. New Media in Public Libraries: a Survey of Current Practices, by James W. Brown. Syracuse, N.Y.: Jeffrey Norton Publishers/Gaylord Bros., Inc., 1976. $12.50, paper. 218p.; index; bibliog. Reports on how public libraries throughout the country are incorporating the new media into their programs. Coverage includes audio-tape and record libraries, 8mm and 16mm film libraries, cable and broadcast television, radio broadcasting, mediamobiles, amateur film and videotape production and film study societies.

3. EPIE Report: Annotated Directory of Parts and Services for Audiovisual Equipment, 1976-77, developed by Association of Audio-Visual Technicians. New York: EPIE Institute, 1976. $20.00, paper. 136pp. Divided into two sections: a directory of brand names and a directory of suppliers.

4. Mediaware: Selection, Operation and Maintenance, by
    Raymond Wyman. 2nd ed. Dubuque, Iowa: Wm. C.
    Brown Co., 1976. $5.95. 229pp.

Chapter 5

PERSONNEL

Laura Murray

A chapter about personnel in a book on establishing audiovisual services in smaller public libraries is about people. It's about individuals--their duties and qualities and how they have to be related to the resources that are likely to be available. The purpose of this chapter is to give you some guidance in making decisions about how many and what kinds of staff will be needed for your audiovisual service.

Our assumptions are that you have already decided that you want to start an audiovisual program and that based on the kinds of considerations discussed in other chapters, you have some idea of the nature and extent of the service you can afford to give to your community.

The ALA's Recommendations for Audiovisual Materials and Services for Small and Medium-Sized Libraries, 1975, in the chapters on Personnel and Resources, relate size of staff to several specifics:

> size of collections
> range of media
> population served
> area served
> hours service is open.

A consideration of these variables leads to these recommendations, on page 17, with regards to personnel:

Each library should have an audiovisual specialist
with a master's degree in library science. A
minimum staff of one full-time professional is
recommended. When more than 200 items of media other than 16mm films are added to the audiovisual collection, at least one full-time assistant
must be added to the staff. Included in audiovisual resources, but not limited to them are the
following: audio tape, educational broadcasting
services, 8mm films, filmstrips, framed art collections, discs, slides and video tape.

Libraries serving a population of 150,000 or less
should have a minimum staff of two for effective
media service.

An audiovisual technician is required for maintenance and repair of audiovisual equipment and
materials. The technician should have specialized
audiovisual vocational training. The technician
should receive the same salary as the other highly
skilled classified personnel serving the region.

The number of additional staff is related to the
number and types of nonprint media collections
and to the area and population served....

An audiovisual program is slightly different from other
services because of the nature of the materials to be handled
and because equipment is involved. There is also a scarcity
of bibliographic tools to aid users and staff in selection.
Even simple aids such as the contents page and index in a
book, which help one in assessing the appropriateness of the
contents, are not available for audiovisual materials. There
is a limited amount of material on any one subject in each
format. Therefore, a much wider variety of user needs has
to be met by fewer items than is usually the case with books.
This fact, coupled with the shortage of bibliographic tools,
places great demands on the staff in an audiovisual program.

Staff needed in a small audiovisual program are usually
of four types: the professional librarian, the clerical assistant,

the audiovisual technician and the pages or occasional help.
The range of duties which have to be carried out in an audiovisual program will influence decisions on not only the number but the types of staff required.

Duties to Be Performed

General duties to be carried out in an audiovisual program
are as follows:

Administration, Organization and Planning	- managing and developing the audiovisual service - supervising staff - problem solving - analyzing user statistics - developing and maintaining support for the service - keeping up to date with developments in the audiovisual field (software, hardware)
Collection Building, Utilization	- searching for, evaluating, selecting, cataloging audiovisual materials - planning film programs for library and community - producing filmographies, publicity announcements, brochures to promote the service
Public Service	- actively promoting the use of audiovisual materials - instructing people in the use of related equipment - providing audiovisual reference service, audiovisual programming service to the public - providing a referral service to existing resources in the community and beyond - providing a preview service for some materials

| Office Duties, | - typing required for building, |

Office Duties,
Statistics
- typing required for building,
  circulating and promoting the
  collections
- circulation routines
- ordering of new materials
- processing new materials
- ordering of supplies
- ordering of replacement footage, etc.

Inspection,
Maintenance
and Repair of
Collections
- regularly scheduled cleaning
  of materials and equipment
- repairing materials and equipment
- ordering of replacement supplies for equipment
- inserting replacement footage
  (16mm film)

This is no more than a general but basic list. These duties all have to be carried out, regardless of the size of the staff, the scope of the collections, or the population served. The extent and complexity of the duties will be influenced by the financial resources available and the nature of the service you propose to give your community.

Distribution of Duties Among Available Staff

The chart on page 81 indicates how the various duties and responsibilities can be shared among the types of staff available in an audiovisual program. We have divided staff into three levels, each level being achieved as an additional type of staff member enters and thus enriches the program.

The chart should be examined in two ways. It indicates the way in which duties can be distributed at any one point in time. It also indicates (see vertical dimension of the chart) how these duties can be redistributed as more staff becomes available.

It is important to keep in mind that the spectrum of

Distribution of duties among available staff in the development
of an audiovisual program in a small public library

	Administration, Organization, Planning	Collection Building, Utilization	Public Service	Office duties, Statistics	Inspection, Maintenance and Repair of Collections & Equipment
Staffing Level 1					
Professional	PPPPPPPPPPPPPPPPPPPPPPPPPPPPPPPPPPPPPPPPPPPPPPPP				
Pages			OOOOOOOOOOOOOOOOOOOOOOOOOOOOOOOOOOOOOOOOOOOOOO		
Staffing Level 2					
Professional	PPPPPPPPPPPPPPPPPPPPPPPPP				
Clerical		CCCCCCCCCCCCCCCCCCCCCCCCCCCCC			
Pages				OOOOOOOOOOOOOOOOOOOOOOOOOOOOOOOO	
Staffing Level 3					
Professional	PPPPPPPPPPPPPPPPPPPPPPP				
Clerical		CCCCCCCCCCCCCCCCCCCCCCC			
Technician			TTTTTTTTTTTTTTTTTTTTTTTTTTTTTTTTTTTTTTTT		
Pages				OOOOOOOOOOOOOOOOOOOOOOOOOOOO	

This chart indicates the way in which the spectrum of duties can be
distributed at any one point in time and how these duties can be redistributed as more staff becomes available.

duties remains the same however many staff members are
available, although naturally the volume of work within each
duty will vary.   Though not recommended, it is probably
possible to carry out the full spectrum of duties at a minimum level of service with some or all staff working part-
time in the audiovisual program.

Levels of Staffing

As illustrated in the chart, the first level of staffing
in the audiovisual program is achieved when a professional
and pages only are available and together perform the range
of duties listed in the spectrum.   Pages will perform some
public service duties but do most of the inspection and maintenance tasks.

The second level is achieved when a clerical assistant
is added to the staff to perform the duties that are found in
the middle of the spectrum, some collection building and
utilization responsibilities, public service, office duties, statistics.   Some inspection and maintenance responsibilities
will also have to be assigned.   At this level, even if more
clerical assistants are hired, the duties of the professional
narrow to exclude office duties and inspection and maintenance,
except in emergencies.   The pages' duties also narrow to exclude public service and office duties, except in emergencies.

The third level is achieved when the audiovisual program becomes large enough to require an audiovisual technician to perform duties such as some public service, office
duties and statistics, as well as inspection, maintenance and
repair of collections and equipment.   A higher quality of
performance in the last three duties mentioned is expected;
for example, greater technical competence in repair of audiovisual equipment.   The professional concentrates on adminis-

tration, organization and planning, collection building and utilization and public service.   The clerical assistant's duties narrow to exclude most maintenance and repair responsibilities.   The pages concentrate on inspection and maintenance duties.   This third level of staffing provides a full complement of staff.

Qualities to Look for in Prospective Staff

Many of the important qualities needed by staff are those common to all good public service staff.   The more technical qualities are necessary simply because of the way in which audiovisual materials are handled.   This latter difference, however, should not be cause for discouragement or held in too much awe.   Many skills considered to be technical and therefore alarming can easily be learned on the job.

We have listed what we consider to be the important and relevant qualities that each of the four types of staff should have.   They should be kept in mind when assessing applicants wishing to participate in the development of your audiovisual program.

The professional librarian must have:

> a vital interest in and commitment to working in this area of public service

> a willingness to learn on-the-job if inexperienced and newly assigned to the audiovisual service

> human relations skills

> administration and management skills

> a knowledge of how audiovisual materials can be used

a knowledge of the audiovisual program and its relationship to the community.

The clerical assistant must have:

an expressed interest in working in the audio-visual program

an ability to work accurately and effectively with a minimum of supervision

a willingness to share duties such as inspection, cleaning, maintenance and repair of materials and equipment.

The audiovisual technician must have:

a knowledge of the basic technical nature of each media format used in the library

a knowledge of the utilization of the equipment; i. e., how it is used, its applications and capabilities, how to operate the equipment and how to teach others

a knowledge of the audiovisual market place, especially local suppliers

a knowledge of audiovisual maintenance and trouble shooting procedures

the willingness to carry out routine tasks such as preventative maintenance, equipment scheduling, handling of parts, supplies and stock

initiative and persistence, because some special skills may have to be learned on the job.

The pages must have:

a positive attitude to the job and about their participation in the audiovisual service

the ability to work well under a minimum of supervision

the potential to develop into a clerical assistant or audiovisual technician.

These qualities are what you should be looking for when assessing prospective staff.

Conclusion

You have your own idea of the nature and the extent of the service you propose to give to your community.

You have knowledge of the ALA recommendations and the variables that will influence your service.

You have a listing of the general duties that must be performed to provide that service.

You have an idea of how the four different types of audiovisual staff can interrelate at different staffing levels during the program's development.

You have some idea of the qualities you are looking for in staff who will be required to perform the necessary duties in the program.

You should now be ready to make decisions about staffing for your proposed audiovisual program.

Chapter 6

PUBLICITY AND PUBLIC RELATIONS

Masha Rudnitzky Porte

It may well be argued that everything that happens in
a public library could be called public relations. The manner in which the most basic library functions are performed--
providing materials in a wide range of subject areas to meet
the needs of a broad spectrum of its community, and having
the materials available when the borrowers want them--can
affect the attitude of the public toward the library. A library whose collections are reasonably comprehensive, in
amounts reasonably adequate, will be used. Where the staff
is pleasant, friendly, knowledgeable, and shows willingness
to be helpful, patrons will respond with warmth toward the
library.

Extra efforts to keep patrons informed of new acquisitions and services can make fans and supporters of the library public. For example, in a small library (whether it
be THE library in a small town or a branch of a large city
library), it is possible for the staff to know personally many
of the patrons, and to be aware of their special needs and
interests. A telephone call or note from the librarian to
let a patron know of some newly received material in his/
her field would earn that patron's gratitude and enhance appreciation of the library.

Certain physical conditions, often taken for granted, may also have a bearing on the patron's inclination to use the library. These include comfortable temperatures and lighting (this makes the staff happy, too, and puts them in a better mood to give good service), clean restrooms, convenient drinking fountains and public telephones. Accessible pencils and slips for writing call numbers from the catalog are routine household items, the absence of which could produce patron irritation. An additional friendly gesture would be to make available, on request, pencil and 8-1/2x11 sheets of paper for patrons who forgot to bring them to use in taking notes in the library.

Location signs about the building should be prominently displayed, attractively designed, and clearly worded. They might help reduce the number of routine questions asked at the service desks, freeing the librarian to answer reference questions.

Even the public catalog can be a public relations tool. When it accurately reflects the library's holdings and their locations, it can prevent such frustration on the part of the user, and may even lead to fuller use of library materials.

All of the foregoing applies to the public library in general, regardless of its size and the format of its materials. Is there, then, some special approach to public relations for audiovisual materials? The answer might be yes-and-no.

In the 1950s, when audiovisual collections in public libraries were just getting on their feet, these materials were themselves considered by library administrations to be public relations tools. They were supposed to attract to the library people who had not used it before and who, through their interest in audiovisual materials, would become con-

verted to books as well. In those days library-sponsored
film programs had to be book-oriented; i. e. , either to present films based on books, or to incorporate into the film
showing perhaps a talk about related books or the distribution of a list of related books. And people who attended
film showings were encouraged--no, tempted--to check out
books. Whether or not the ploy succeeded has not, to my
knowledge, been determined.

By the mid-1960s, audiovisual collections in public
libraries were becoming an accepted concept, and at least
lip service was given to the "integration" of print and nonprint materials. Such integration seemed most likely with
recordings (disc or tape), and possibly also with 8mm films.
Their cost approximates that of books and their use, like
that of books, is mainly on a personal, non-scheduled basis.
It was more likely, then, that small libraries would be able
to provide their own collections of recordings for their patrons. The more expensive 16mm films were less likely
to be part of the small public library's holdings.

In recent years, spurred by funding from Federal
and State sources, there has been an increase in regional
systems of library cooperation. This has provided small
libraries with access to 16mm films, for their own programming and/or to loan to their patrons. What kind of public
relations/publicity programs can and should these small libraries undertake to encourage the use of nonprint materials,
to have them considered a valid and integral part of the library, and to obtain public, government, and administrative
support for their inclusion in the library's activities?

A quick, informal survey in the form of a questionnaire was conducted among the 45 member libraries of the
Northeast Texas Library System (NETLS), the writer's home

territory, and among the 32 libraries of the adjacent Fort
Worth Major Resource System.   Twenty-six NETLS members
responded, while 21 replies were received from the Fort
Worth group, about half of whom, however, were not participating in any audiovisual programs.   Because areas served
by these libraries vary in size from just over 2,000 population to 120,000, and because audiovisual service is relatively
new for most of these libraries, no clear pattern of public
relations/publicity activities emerged from the responses.

But they did produce one sure conclusion: to provide
audiovisual materials and services, and to promote their use
effectively, someone in the library has to want to do it.   It
may be the librarian, the library board or a member of the
board; whoever it is must have the strong desire and the
ability to spark interest in others.

A library in a town of 36,000 people stated it has so
far had no luck in interesting the community in audiovisual
materials and services.   In another town of only 10,000 in-
habitants, where the library consists of one cluttered, murky
room in the County Court House, film showings and other
events are held in a court room, in City Hall, in local
churches, and they are well attended.   One library in a town
of 7,000 people says it has no funds, space, or personnel
for non-book materials; another in the same size community
borrows free films from various sources and shows them
twice a month at children's story hours, once a month to
adults at night screenings.   The difference is in the motiva-
tion.

All of the libraries queried which offer audiovisual
services use some sort of publicity devices to make their
publics aware of their availability.   Posters and flyers in
the library are routine.   Many libraries also ask business

firms in the community to display their posters, and receive
good cooperation. Announcements placed outside of the library can reach people who do not frequent the library. Good
places to display posters and leave flyers are grocery stores,
beauty salons, cleaning establishments, laundromats, drug
stores--wherever there is much people-traffic.

Many libraries use their mailing lists to good effect.
They send announcements of audiovisual programs, lists of
new acquisitions, and invitations to participate in library activities. This is another way of reaching non-users, and
often making library patrons of them.

Periodic mailings to organizations, letting them know
of newly available films and recordings in their special interest area, win friends for the library and attract borrowers to it. Special mailings announcing film programs in
which particular groups would be interested are an effective
method of drawing audiences. Mailings can consist of a
single letter or flyer asking that the information be announced
to each group's membership, or quantities of mailers to be
passed out to the members. Flyers can be sent to the
schools in quantity, to be placed in the teachers' mail boxes.
Teachers are not only invited to events, but are asked to
bring their students or to recommend that students attend.

Mailing lists can be compiled from many sources.
One way might be to have new borrowers registering for
library cards list on their applications any subjects of particular interest to them. Another is to have people attend-
ing film showings complete an attendance card to be kept on.
file at the library. County Councils of Social Agencies can
provide lists of organizations concerned with particular fields
of community health and welfare. Chambers of Commerce
can suggest names of businesses and industrial firms. A

member of one group often voluntarily mentions the names
of related groups. And so the list grows and the categories
grow.

Special mailings can be tied to current events. In
this writer's own experience, such a device was used as long
as twenty years ago. A newspaper article discussing the
formation of a city government committee to study urban re-
newal was clipped, reproduced, and mailed to selected civic
groups with a note about the availability at the library of the
then-current film, BALTIMORE PLAN. Even if such a mailing does not initially generate a single film request, it makes
recipients aware that the library can supply films to meet
their special needs and concerns.

The community college, small private college, or
branch of a state university make excellent targets for library information. As with public schools, posters can be
placed on college bulletin boards, flyers can be put in faculty
mail boxes and in dormitories. (Many colleges now have
their own active film programs, which build audiences for
this kind of event. The library can cooperate and do itself
a service by avoiding duplication of types and content of film
showings.)

Establishing good relations with members of college
faculties, business people and professional people in the community can be mutually beneficial to the audiovisual librarian
and these contacts. They can be invited to preview films in
their special areas of knowledge, lending their expertise to
the evaluation of the way in which the subject is presented.
At the same time, they are made aware of the library's
holdings in their field which may be useful in their work.
In addition, these specialists can make known to the audiovisual librarian new materials in their subjects, announced

in their professional journals, of which the librarian may
not be aware.   Virtually every community, even the smallest, has
its own newspaper, even if it comes out only twice or once
a week. In most cases, the newspaper is glad to use items
about library activities. Often the town librarian has a
regular column in the newspaper, through which such information can be conveyed. If not, and if the librarian would
like to undertake such a column, the newspaper editor or
publisher could be approached on the subject. Failing this,
the library could regularly supply news to the editor or local
reporter/columnist.

The good will and cooperation of the newspaper can
be maintained by, first, knowing and adhering to press dead-
lines. This also helps the library by insuring that the news
items appear at the most advantageous time in advance of a
program. It is helpful to know the editor or reporter personally, to find out the publication's requirements as to format in which items are to be submitted (usually typewritten
double-spaced wide-margined stories), or what kind of a
slant on a story is preferred. The newspaper staff can also
sometimes alert the librarian to a situation to which the library can relate its programming or announcement of available material, or even help the librarian's approach to the
city government for library funding, building space, or other
needs.

If a newspaper carries a regular calendar of local
events, the library's programs should be included. But
there should, in addition, be press releases in greater de-
tail about the films to be shown, the persons to introduce
them (if any), or any other special aspect of the program.

The first story would, of course, be the announcement

that the library is initiating audiovisual service, either in the form of materials to be checked out or of a series of programs in the library. The story could disclose plans for increasing the collections, subject areas to be covered, rules for borrowing, etc. Or, if materials (especially films) are obtained from a regional source or through a film circuit, the manner in which the library will make them available to local residents can be outlined. Such an initial release can then be followed by regular stories about new acquisitions or coming programs or tie-ins with local or national events.

It is important to remember that stories sent to the newspapers should be truly newsworthy. When appropriate, they could be accompanied by an eye-catching photograph, preferably an 8 x 10" glossy print.

Townspeople feel closer to their library, more a part of the institution, when given a glimpse of its inner working. So newsworthy items might include some behind-the-scenes stories. Plans for the future, such as enlargement of the collections in some significant way, affiliation with a regional system or cooperative, acquisition of new equipment, space changes or needs, fund-raising activities to fill some of these future plans and needs--all might merit some public notice. Staff activities are also of interest to the public.

Changes in staff, additions of positions, recognition of staff members by appointment to state, regional or national library organization offices or committees; programs of these organizations in which staff members participate; attendance at conventions, workshops, film festivals--each is worth an item in the local press. They are especially effective when they show how staff activities can help improve service to the community.

A regular newspaper release could be a filmography

and/or discography on specific subject areas. When connected
to some current event or situation, such lists are newsworthy
because of their timeliness. Printed or mimeographed copies
of these lists could also be available in the library for patrons to pick up.

Another regular feature could be periodic lists of new
acquisitions of audiovisual materials, or selected titles in
various formats. These could be combined with brief reviews of some outstanding works. Or the reviews could be
a separate kind of release for the press.

Television is not quite so accessible to small communities as are other information media. But if television
in a nearby area city reaches the small community, the library could approach the station's program or public service
director with proposals for submitting information. Television and radio stations are obliged by the FCC to devote a
certain amount of air time to public interest broadcasts, so
the library has some opportunity at least to compete with
other organizations and institutions for this free time. Television can use short spot announcements (20-, 30-, or 60-
second items) of library programs and services. A television crew could be invited to the library to record some
special event, such as an anniversary celebration, the opening of an exhibit, the installation of some new equipment,
and similar highlights. One library which replied to the
writer's questionnaire mentioned sending spot announcements
to be used on a cable television time-weather service.

Radio offers much wider opportunities for libraries
at this time. Many small communities have local radio stations which would accept spot announcements of library news.
They could also use library staff for periodic film or recording or book reviews, or talks about library services,
or other educational programs.

In preparing information for the electronic media, it
is important to know the public served by the station(s), their
interests, educational levels, listening habits. It is also
good to know the most effective broadcast times. Armed
with this knowledge, the librarian can tailor the promotion
accordingly.

Sometimes, however, it doesn't hurt to break such a
rule by sending news randomly. One library surveyed reported that the "cultured" members of its community considered the local radio station "hicktown, " but the library
message got across effectively and produced the desired results in terms of increased attendance and usage.

Samples of spot announcements and ideas for their
content are occasionally available from the National Library
Week office. They can be adapted to fit the needs of the
local library. One of this writer's favorite examples of a
timely announcement was submitted by one of the Texas libraries answering the questionnaire:

> If you missed the Ford-Carter debate, come to
> the _____ Public Library to see a videotape
> replay. The debate, in its entirety, can be
> viewed any time during library hours. For fur-
> ther information, call the librarian at _____.

The same library has issued news releases about the
availability of filmstrip-cassette kits on the metric system,
the acquisition of language study cassettes, and a potpourri
of new acquisitions in a variety of subjects, as well as spot
announcements of children's film showings.

Having touched on the uses of today's major communications media, it is important not to overlook an old standard practice of librarians, one which remains valid still:
the school visit. Several librarians who responded to the
survey included the school visit as one of their publicity/

public relations techniques. Usually librarians visiting the classroom or the school library give book talks, display books, and invite students to the public library. Librarians who wish to emphasize audiovisual materials could show a film, talk about certain categories of library films which would be of interest to students, or about film making, and invite students to the library's film showings and to listen to recordings, use filmstrip-cassette kits, and other materials.

Other "personal appearances" by the librarian could include being a guest speaker for meetings of various community organizations. In communities large and small, librarians are in demand to appear on club programs. The talk could be tailored to the group's field of interest, or it could be a discussion of the library's services, its role in the community. The talk could be combined with the showing of a film related to the organization's concerns. This writer recently combined a talk about the film library's services with the showing of the film, CITIZEN KANE, at a meeting of the local chapter of a professional journalists' society. Because the film's protagonist is supposed to be patterned after the newspaper publisher, William Randolph Hearst, the journalists were especially interested in seeing this classic motion picture. The program was rounded out with a slide show of Hearst's estate, San Simeon, presented by a member of the journalists' society.

In a reversal of the librarian's "personal appearance" role, the library which has the facilities could encourage groups to tour the institution. One library in the survey group reported that it welcomes daily tour groups, mainly from schools, and that each tour includes the showing of a film. Librarians following this practice could show a film

on a subject and understanding level suited to the visitors.
Or the film could be about the work of the library, or about
the function of libraries in general, or about how to use
some of the tools in the library.   Increasing numbers of libraries are making their own films, or having them made,
detailing aspects of their operations.   It is an expensive venture, but it is worth investigating ways to cut costs on such
a project.

Exhibitors of theatrical (i. e. , commercial) movies
and stage presentations--in fact, everyone in the entertainment business--spend a considerable amount of money on advertising their offerings.   Whether their newspaper ads are
one inch or a full page, the advertisers also rely very
heavily on word-of-mouth advertising: people who have seen
and enjoyed the movie or play or musical show tell others
and recommend attendance.

So, it seems, do small town public libraries, many
of whom, replying to the questionnaire, included this factor
in their lists of publicity devices.   Some of them commented
that especially in small towns, word-of-mouth can be a successful method of making known a library's programs, collections, and services.

Some libraries use word-of-mouth in a planned manner, by conducting or overseeing telephone campaigns to
promote interest in certain programs.   This is a familiar
device, used by candidates for political office and by poll-
takers of all kinds.   In a small community it becomes all
the more effective because more people know one another
and can make their persuasiveness a personal matter.

So far we have touched on the library's environment,
staff, collections, programs, and publicity campaigns as
parts of its over-all public relations efforts.   What other

avenues should be considered to bring the library, and in particular its audiovisual services, to the attention of the community?

It should be explained, as preface, that most of the libraries which responded to the writer's questionnaire are extremely small, many of them having only one librarian on the staff, and sometimes only a part-time librarian at that. Some have one or two part-time clerks, many rely on volunteer help. In these instances, where audiovisual services are offered, everyone on the staff does some of the work, and the librarian does whatever collection building is done. A few libraries reported having some ten to 20 staff members, including one or two librarians. Only three libraries reported 30 to 40 staff members, with one person assigned to the audiovisual service.

So the questionnaire yielded little or no information as to what is actually being done in some aspects of public relations. What follows, therefore, are suggestions of what might be done by smaller libraries which are still large enough to have a person responsible primarily for audio-visual materials selection and management.

In order to gain support for audiovisual services, the librarian should see to it that the library director is kept fully aware of audiovisual activities. Aside from and in between the regular reports (usually monthly) of circulation statistics, materials acquired, programs presented, and other facts, the library director should receive copies of filmographies and discographies published, of publicity releases and press clippings, and of new acquisitions lists.

The library director, each member of the library board, the mayor and members of the City Council should receive notices of audiovisual programs, with a brief note inviting their presence. They may not be able to attend all, or any, of the programs; nor even be interested in them personally. But at least they are kept informed of the service the library is offering, and will be able to act on proposals affecting the audiovisual service.

Filmographies, discographies, and new acquisitions lists should also be sent to library trustees and to the City administration, either at the time they are issued, or, at the discretion of the library director, along with the library's report to those governing agencies.

Filmographies and discographies should be sent also to selected lists of individuals and groups with special interest in the subjects of the lists. Several libraries responding to the questionnaire reported that such mailings resulted in at least initially heavy use of the materials.

It is useful to know the director's special likes and interests, personal and professional. When the audiovisual librarian receives information about new materials (films, especially) in areas of the director's concern, the flyers, reviews, or whatever form the information takes, could be called to the director's attention, with an offer to request the film(s) for preview if the director wishes to screen them. This not only gives the director access to information about a subject of concern; it also makes the director aware that information is available in audiovisual format as well as in print, and boosts the value of the audiovisual service.

To underline the chief librarian's awareness, he/she should be regularly furnished with copies of film preview schedules and invited to attend the screenings. It may not often be possible for the director to preview, but he/she will be kept aware of the kinds of films being considered for purchase and of the amount of previewing being done. This

should give the director some understanding of the needs of
the audiovisual service and make him/her more authoritative
in trying to support those needs before trustees and City officials.

    With the approval of the director, members of the
library board could also be invited to film previews. This
could take the form of a blanket invitation to the board to
attend whenever possible, with some idea of the preview
schedule. Or individual board members could be especially
asked to screen films within their known areas of interest
or expertise. This not only keeps them aware of audiovisual
operations, but gives the library the benefit of their knowledge of a given subject by having them evaluate the film's
presentation of that subject.

    In cases where the library does not purchase films
of its own but previews jointly with a cooperative or a regional film service, the audiovisual librarian could ask the
library director to accompany him/her to the joint preview
sessions. In this way the director could gain insight into
the effects of the library's participation in cooperative audiovisual services, and again, could become more authoritative
in seeking support for that cooperation.

    The library director should be immediately informed
of unusual circumstances in connection with audiovisual services: a film or recording or other medium used in a
unique way by a patron; an interesting reference question
answered through the use of library materials; a group or
individual helped because of special materials or reference
tools; significant gifts from patrons or community groups.
This information helps emphasize to the director that audiovisual services are performed for people, and that people do
appreciate their availability.

Because film, in particular, works well in a group
context (better, perhaps, than other library material), it
makes a natural stepping-stone from the library to community organizations of all kinds. The library's audiovisual
operation can offer many valuable services to groups, but
by virtue of such services, the audiovisual librarian can ask
for reciprocal favors from the community. In fact, help
from the community ultimately reverts to the people's benefit in terms of improved and/or increased services.

To recapitulate, community contacts already mentioned include mailings, telephone campaigns, posters outside
the library, school visit, speaking and/or film showing for
group meetings, library tours with film showings.

Those libraries with the means to do so (staff and
physical facilities) could make their meeting rooms available
to community organizations for the showing of films at their
meetings, and/or for talks about audiovisual services. For
groups meeting outside the library, special audiovisual programs could be arranged, as touched on in foregoing para-
graphs.

A close relationship can result from joint program
planning by the library and one or more community groups.
In this writer's experience, two such joint ventures stand
out. One was a whole season of cooperation with the Dallas
Council on World Affairs in the showing of films. At that
time the library had no meeting room and the Council had a
500-seat theater. So the Council provided the room, the
projector, and the projectionist. The library planned the
programs, released press announcements, wrote program
notes, engaged speakers to introduce the films, and collected
attendance cards. The series provided an excellent means
of gaining experience and an audience for the following year,

when the library moved into its new building and a film
series was begun in its own auditorium.   It was the beginning of the very successful eighteen-year film series, "Focus
on Film."

Another major cooperative venture was a two-day film
workshop with the Anti-Defamation League of B'nai B'rith,
held in the library's conference room and showing films on
"brotherhood." Films were provided by both the library and
the ADL; the workshop booklet and program notes were designed by the audiovisual librarian and a member of ADL,
and all arrangements were jointly planned and executed.

These kinds of undertakings, besides being of intrin-
sic worth in bringing significant materials to the public, are
also very valuable in building good will for the library and
broadening its contacts with the community.   The "brotherhood" workshop still has occasional repercussions, in the
form of requests for some of the films shown then and for
other films, coming from organizations whose representa-
tives had attended that workshop so many years ago.

Programs could be co-sponsored with academic institutions, business groups, professional organizations, churches,
and others.   Developing friendships with these groups could
pave the way for the library to ask for their cooperation in
publicizing the library's services.   Already noted has been
the willingness of businesses to display library posters.   But
there's more that groups can do.

Banks and utility companies could use library stuffers
in their mailings of statements and bills, respectively.

Special interest groups could contribute funds for the
purchase of films and other audiovisual materials in their
particular subject areas.   The writer remembers with gratitude the gift from a church day school of money to buy a

children's film, because the school had used so many from
the library's collection.   This was an unsolicited gift, but
there should be no hesitancy in suggesting to a group for
which the library has been an extensive source of audiovisual
materials and service, that it help increase the audiovisual
collection in the area of that group's interest.   One of the
larger libraries responding to the questionnaire noted that
two of its 16mm film projectors were gifts from the community: one from the local Jaycees, the other from a nursery
school.

The possibilities are endless, bounded only by the
imagination, innovativeness, and aggressiveness of the audiovisual librarian.

The reader who has remained with this essay thus far
may question the feasibility of a small library's pursuing so
many avenues of public relations.   But take heart; they are
not as complex as they may seem.   Some of the activities
suggested are traditional for libraries and are done routinely,
but here they are proposed for audiovisual services rather
than just for books.   Other suggestions may require a little
extra time and effort.   How to gain the time?

One method for libraries with small staffs is to use
volunteers for routine library duties--paging, clerical, typing,
filing, even some circulation and processing operations.   One
library responding to the survey reported using volunteers
for story hours.   It might be possible to enlist the help of
retired persons for both the routine tasks and to tell the library story to the public.   The Friends of the Library can
perform invaluable service in raising funds, encouraging
gifts from groups and individuals, lobbying for a new building or other library needs.   Friends of the Library and
other volunteers can help distribute posters and flyers, and
do similar errands.

And to win friends for the library, it's again back to
the basics--providing the highest possible quality of materials
and services.

The foregoing is a collection of random thoughts compiled principally from personal experience and observation,
and to some extent from responses to the informal questionnaire sent to a limited number and kinds of public libraries.
Most of what has been written does not apply exclusively to
the audiovisual situation, but could certainly be adapted to
it. Little or no previous writing has been found which re-
lates directly and solely to audiovisual publicity and public
relations. Perhaps this piece will be a beginning, pointing
the direction to more extensive coverage of the subject in
the future.

This essay has dealt mainly with general aspects of
public library publicity and public relations, with only occasional hints at specific activities. For more concrete ideas
and some practical how-to's, some further reading may be
suggested, although, again, it does not relate directly to
audiovisual services.

A 1953 American Library Association pamphlet, Promotion Ideas for Public Libraries, by Sarah Leslie Wallace,
today seems dated and elementary. There is, however, a
chapter on special collections which might benefit smaller
libraries looking for ideas on how to build and publicize
films and recordings collections. Another chapter deals in-
formatively with how to solicit gifts. The reader may or
may not wish to follow the suggestions exactly; they may,
however, engender other ideas and methods of collection
promotion and gift solicitation.

Betty Rice's Public Relations for Public Libraries;
Creative Problem Solving (H. W. Wilson, 1972) deals with

libraries in general, just touching on film programming.
But there are some worthwhile thoughts on the philosophy
and techniques of public relations in this book.
Problems in Library Public Relations, by Cosette
Kies (R. R. Bowker, 1974) covers all kinds of libraries and
all kinds of relations--staff, patrons, trustees, students,
etc. Each chapter contains a case history of a given situation, in both narrative and dialogue form, followed by the
author's comments on how the case was handled and sometimes how it might have been done. There are some nug-
gets here, if one looks for them.

Perhaps one of the most helpful works is Steve Sher-
man's ABC's of Library Promotion (Scarecrow Press, 1971),
in which the author spends three chapters on the philosophy
of library public relations and nine more on the practicali-
ties of publicity and public relations: how to deal with newspapers, how to prepare materials for radio and television,
even how to make one's own films and slides. The final
chapters offer ideas for use by the various types of libraries.
Again, there is nothing here specifically for promoting audiovisual services, but much that can be applied to the audiovisual operation.

Maybe this is the time to recognize that audiovisual
services can, should--must--be integrated with over-all library services; that promotion, publicity, and public relations for the whole library must include attention to special
collections such as the audiovisual materials. But even if
this goal is attained, there are special things which can be
done in behalf of audiovisual operations.

And perhaps these old-time administrators were right
after all: that audiovisual materials and services are themselves excellent public relations tools.

Chapter 7

DEFINITIONS AND GLOSSARY

Wesley A. Doak

ABSTRACT
A factual summary giving the significant content of a unit of publication (e.g., a film, a scientific or scholarly paper, a technical report, a patent). It may accompany the full paper when originally published, or it may be issued separately with a citation referring to the original publication.

ACCESSION NUMBER
The number given to a work in the order of its addition to the collection.

ACCOMPANYING MATERIAL
Guides, notes, leaflets, audio and visual material issued with the work to convey its concepts more completely.

ACCREDITATION
An official decision by an agency having official authority, that, in its judgment, the unit has met the established standards of quality. Accreditation may or may not have legal status.

ACCREDITED LIBRARY SCHOOL
A library school approved by the American Library Association, the authorized accrediting agency for the programs of library education at the graduate level.

ACOUSTICAL RECORDING
Recordings made before the advent of electrical techniques, when the music or speech was channeled through an inverted megaphone rather than a microphone.

ACQUISITION
The area of library service comprising the obtaining of

library materials by purchase, exchange, or gift, together with the maintenance of the necessary records of these additions.

ACQUISITIONS DEPARTMENT
The administrative unit in charge of acquiring books, periodicals, audio visuals, and other materials by purchase, exchange, or gift, and of keeping the necessary records of these additions. Sometimes referred to as order department.

ADAPTATION
A new version of a work, frequently modified for a purpose or use other than that for which the original work was intended.

ADDED ENTRY
An entry, in a cataloging record, in addition to the main entry under which a work is represented in a catalog.

ADMINISTRATION
(1) The active management of a library, library program, or library system. (2) The area of library service comprising the determination of policy and program, financial management, personnel coordination and supervision, and public relations for a library or library system.

ADMINISTRATIVE UNIT
Any independent library, or a group of libraries, under a single director or a single administration.

ADULT EDUCATION
The acquisition of knowledge by those beyond school age through regularly organized programs which have as their purpose the development of skills, knowledge, habits, or attitudes.

ADVERTISING BROCHURES
Informational pamphlets issued by commercial firms as advertising for their products.

ADVISORY SERVICES
Counsel rendered to individuals, groups, organizations, institutions, libraries, and library systems, and to governmental bodies in the use, establishment, administration, and financing of library service and of library buildings and equipment.

AECT
 The Association for Educational Communications and Technology (formerly the Department of Audiovisual Instruction
 of the National Education Association) is a national organization which deals in audiovisual instruction and technology, related resources, and those who use them.
 AECT is headquartered in Washington, D. C.

AFFILIATED LIBRARY
 A member of a library system. The affiliated library
 has its own governance and is not administered by a central library, as is the case with, for example, a branch
 library.

AIDE
 A person with few or no special skills who performs simple tasks usually under the supervision of a technician or
 specialist. An aide's tasks are specified in terms of a
 specific product and have clear directions or instructions
 for performance.

ALA
 The American Library Association is a major organization for librarians in the United States and Canada, with
 headquarters in Chicago. Many committees in ALA are
 concerned with, and work directly with audiovisual matters.

ALBUM
 A popular, but very general, term for an audiorecording
 including the actual recording and the accompanying ma-
 terial(s).

ALLOTMENT
 The amount allotted for a certain period or purpose.

ALPHANUMERIC
 A character set that pertains to letters, digits, and
 usually other characters such as punctuation marks.

AMERICAN LIBRARY ASSOCIATION See ALA

AMERICAN NATIONAL STANDARD CODE FOR INFORMATION
INTEREXCHANGE (ASCII)
 The standard code, using a coded character set consisting of 7-bit coded characters (8 bits including parity
 check), used for information interchange among data

processing systems, communication systems, and associated equipment. The ASCII set consists of control
characters and graphic characters. Synonymous with
USASCIL

AMERICAN NATIONAL STANDARDS INSTITUTE (ANSI)
An organization responsible for the development of standards in the field of librarianship.

AMPLIFIER
An electronic component that can modify the sound on a
projector, phonograph, etc., to the desired listening
tone and loudness level.

AMPLITUDE MODULATION
The system of radio transmission based on varying the
amplitude of the power output while the frequency remains the same (also called AM).

ANAMORPHIC LENS
A lens composed of elements which, when used, com-
presses a wide image onto a standard frame of film.
When used as a projection lens, it returns the image to
its proper width. The best known anamorphic process
is "CinemaScope."

ANIMATION
The film process which gives motion to inanimate objects
or drawings by shooting them one frame at a time. The
best examples of this type of film are cartoons.

ANNOTATION
A note accompanying an entry in a bibliography, reading
list, or catalog--intended to describe, explain, or evaluate the publication to which it refers.

ANNUAL
A serial publication issued regularly once a year, as an
annual report or proceedings of an organization; or, a
yearly publication that reviews events or developments
during a year, in descriptive or statistical form, or
both, sometimes limited to a special field. Also includes annals, yearbooks, etc.

APERTURE CARD
A data card with a rectangular hole or holes specifically
prepared for the mounting or insertion therein of microfilm.

APPROPRIATION
An authorization granted by a legislative body to make expenditures and to incur obligations for specific purposes.

ARCHIVES
The organized body of records made or received in connection with the transaction of its affairs by a government or a governmental agency, an institution, organization, or establishment, or a family or individual, and preserved for record purposes in its custody or that of its legal successors.

AREA OF SERVICE
A library term applying to the geographical area and the residents thereof, to whom the library offers its services free of charge and from which (or on behalf of which) the library derives income.

ART PRINT
A reproduction of a two-dimensional work of art, generally listed without instructional text.

ASSOCIATION FOR EDUCATIONAL COMMUNICATIONS AND TECHNOLOGY See AECT

AUDIO COMPARATOR
A monophonic, dual-track audiotape recorder with provision for the user to record on one track and play back both tracks. It is used primarily in foreign language training so that the learner can record his voice and then compare his language facility with the instructor's.

AUDIO CONSOLE
A rank, bench, or desk-type structure equipped with devices for use in processing audio signals during recording, playback, or radio broadcast of audiorecordings or live performances.

AUDIO MIXER
A device which permits the combining of two or more input signals simultaneously into one audio system, subject to various controls of the mixer.

AUDIO RECORDINGS
Materials on which only sounds are stored and can be reproduced (played back) mechanically and/or electronically.

AUDIOCARD
A thin card with a strip of $\frac{1}{4}$-inch audiotape across the bottom of its width (usually 12 inches or less). The sounds recorded on tape are usually ten seconds or less in length. Space is provided above the audiotape for pictures or words.

AUDIODISC
A disc, usually of vinyl, in which is impressed a continuous fine spiral groove. As the audiodisc revolves, it causes a stylus to vibrate and produce electrical signals which are converted to sound. (Also called phonograph record, phonodisc, sound recording, phonorecord and variants of these terms.)

AUDIOLINGUAL METHOD
An approach to foreign language teaching that considers languages a set of habits that are mastered by repetition, drills, and overlearning. Listening and speaking are considered the central skills that are later followed by reading and writing.

AUDIOPAGE
A sheet with visual information on one side and a magnetic coating capable of recording and playing back sound on the other side.

AUDIOROLL
A roll of paper or other material containing a pattern of holes that actuate the sound producing devices. Example: pianorolls.

AUDIOSLIDE
A 2-by-2 inch slide with a brief audiorecording on magnetic materials on the slide mount. The audioslide requires a special projector.

AUDIOSLIDE PROJECTOR
A slide projector which projects audioslides and plays the sound on the slide frame. Audioslide projectors often have provision for recording sound on the audioslide.

AUDIOTAPE CARTRIDGE, RECORDED
A permanently encased single reel of audiotape which has the ends joined together to form a continuous loop that provides playback without rewinding. (Also called Audiocassette.)

AUDIOTAPE CASSETTE, RECORDED
A permanently encased two-reel system of recorded audiotape. The tape is usually 150 mils wide and usually recorded at 1-7/8 inches per second. (Also called Audiocassette.)

AUDIOTAPE DUPLICATOR
A device used to transfer the audio signal from one audiotape to another. Duplicators usually make the transfer to one or more copies at speeds much faster than real time or ordinary playback speeds. It may duplicate audiotapes on reels, cassettes, or cartridges.

AUDIOTAPE PLAYER
A unit which can play back recorded audiotapes but which is not capable of recording. It contains a head for playback, amplifiers, and tape transport mechanisms. (Also called playback unit or audio player.)

AUDIOTAPE PLAYER, CARTRIDGE
An audiotape player which plays only audiotapes in cartridges. (Also called cartridge player.)

AUDIOTAPE PLAYER, CASSETTE
An audiotape player which plays only audiotapes in cassettes. (Also called cassette player.)

AUDIOTAPE PLAYER, REEL
An audiotape player which plays only audiotapes on reels.

AUDIOTAPE, RECORDED
A strip of magnetic tape on one side of which electrical signals are recorded which can be converted to reproduce sound. While audiotapes range in size from 150 mils to 1 inch, the most common size in library applications is 150 mils (in cassettes) and $\frac{1}{4}$-inch (reels).

AUDIOTAPE RECORDER
A unit which can record and play back sound on audiotape. It contains heads for erasing, recording, and playback; amplifiers; and tape transport mechanisms. The recorder may be monophonic, stereophonic, or four-channel and may have provisions for comparison of channels. (Also called tape recorder, recorder/reproducer.)

AUDIOTAPE RECORDER, CARTRIDGE
An audiotape recorder which uses only audiotape in cartridges.

AUDIOTAPE RECORDER, CASSETTE
An audiotape recorder which uses only audiotapes in cassettes.

AUDIOTAPE REEL
A narrow, flanged spool for audiotape. The reel is usually 3, 5, or 7 inches in diameter.

AUDIOTAPE REEL, RECORDED
An audiotape which uses only audiotapes on reels. (Also called Reel-to-Reel Tape or Audioreel.)

AUDIOVISUAL
Communications resources which rely on a device for transmission, reproduction, or enlargement to be effectively utilized or understood. Excluded are print and print substitutes, such as microform, but included are art works and objects.

AUDIOVISUAL AREA
An area in a library, or serving as an adjunct to a library, designed or provided with special equipment for audiovisual materials, storage, screening, and listening.

AUDIOVISUAL MATERIALS
Materials, such as audio and video recordings, transparencies, slides, motion picture films and filmstrips, which require the use of special equipment in order to be seen or heard. Does not include microforms.

AUDIOVISUAL SPECIALIST
A staff member of a library engaged in activities related to the acquisition, use and care of audiovisual equipment and to the techniques of presentation through the use of audiovisual equipment and materials.

AUDIOWIRE
Magnetized steel wire capable of recording and playing back sound.

AUTHOR (CREATOR)
The person(s) or corporate body chiefly responsible for the creation of the intellectual or artistic content of a work.

AUTOMATIC CHANGER
A device on which more than one recording may be played without interruption.

AUTOMATIC DATA PROCESSING (ADP)
The use of machines and devices in the storing of individual items of information in a form by which they may be rapidly and accurately retrieved, processed, and reproduced as single-line items, as lists of items, or in desired combinations with other items.

AUTOMATIC RETRIEVAL UNITS
Devices or systems which can locate a specific item automatically from a file of data.

AUTOMATIC THREADING
The process used for film and other devices (cameras, projectors, or inspection equipment) which requires only insertion of the leader into the machine to engage the film in sprockets or rollers for transmission.

AUTOMATION
(1) The implementation of processes by automatic means.
(2) The theory, art, or technique of making a process more automatic.
(3) The application of methods of rendering processes automatic, self-moving, or self-controlling.
(4) The conversion of a procedure, a process, or equipment to automatic operation.

BATCH PROCESSING
(1) The technique of executing a set of computer programs so that each is completed before the next program of the set is started.
(2) The sequential input of computer programs or data.
(3) Loosely, the execution of computer programs serially.

BIBLIOGRAPHIC INFORMATION INTERCHANGE FORMAT
A format for the exchange, rather than the local processing, of bibliographic records. (The terms "bibliographic information interchange format," "information interchange format," and "interchange format" are used interchangeably.)

BIBLIOGRAPHIC RECORD
The specific and unique description of any recorded item.

BIBLIOGRAPHIC SERVICE
Those activities relating to the selection and dissemination of information from a specialized "literature." These activities may be undertaken in anticipation of users' re-

quests or in response to requests on a single or recur-
ring basis.

BIBLIOGRAPHIC UNIT
A defined body of recorded information and the artifact
on which it is recorded, for example, a film, a videotape, a book, chapter of a book, map, cuneiform tablet,
digital magnetic tape file, song (sheet music), and song
(phonograph record). A bibliographic unit may be part
of a larger bibliographic unit (for example, the chapter
as part of a book, which in turn may be part of a
series). A single author or subject heading authority
record is also a bibliographic unit. (Note: It is assumed that the originators follow a set of rules or
guidelines which define, for the originating source,
what is to be treated as a bibliographic unit.)

BIBLIOGRAPHIC VOLUME
A unit of publication distinguished from other units by
having its own title page, half title, cover title, or port-
folio title; for periodicals, the publisher's volume; for
film, unique credits on opening or closing frames.

BIBLIOGRAPHY
A list of references to library materials organized for
a particular use or relating to a particular subject.

BICYCLING
A method of routing films sent for special programming
or evaluation to a group of selected locations. Often
the arrangements are made with the selected libraries
by a main library, service center or commercial firm.
There may or may not be a fee, but the films return
to the original source at the end of the routing.

BLURB
A brief summary of the content of a work.

BOOKING
Reserving materials for a specific person or group at
a specific place on a specific date. Reserving an item
means holding it so that the patron can pick it up.
Booking is much more specific and can include shipping
or delivery to a patron; it must always be done in advance.

BOOKMOBILE
An automobile truck especially equipped to carry books

and other library materials and serve as a traveling branch library. See also Mediamobile.

BRAILLE MATERIALS
Library materials for the visually handicapped using a system of embossed print.

BRANCH LIBRARY
(1) An auxiliary library with separate quarters, a permanent basic collection of resources, a permanent staff, and a regular schedule, but administered from a central unit.
(2) In college and university libraries, a branch consists of a special area or subject collection of library materials, serviced by its own staff. It is usually located on the same campus as the main library and is centrally administered. See also Departmental Library, Extension Center Library.

BUDGET
An estimate of proposed expenditures for a given period or purpose ... the proposed means of financing them.

BUILDING EFFICIENCY
A means of determining the efficiency of the design of a library, and sometimes used to make initial estimates of the gross area of a building, thereby estimating the probable cost. Building efficiency is stated as a formula:

$$E = \frac{\text{assignable area}}{\text{gross area}} \times 100$$

in which the result is a percentage. Thus, if a building has 50,000 square feet of assignable area and 75,000 square feet of gross area, its efficiency is stated as:

$$\frac{50,000}{75,000} \times 100 = 66.6 \text{ per cent}$$

This procedure is useful for comparing the efficiency of different libraries only if all measurements of net assignable area and gross area are made by the same methods.

BULLETIN
A publication, usually numbered, issued at regular intervals by a government department, a society, or an institution.

BYTE
A sequence of adjacent binary digits operated upon as a unit and usually shorter than a computer word.

CALL NUMBER
The combination of numbers and/or letters which indicate the subject classification of a work and its location on the shelf.

CAPITAL EXPENDITURES
Expenditures which result in the acquisition of or addition to fixed assets, e. g. , building sites, new buildings and building additions, equipment (including initial book stock), and furnishings for new or expanded buildings. Excludes investments for capital appreciation, and replacement and repair of existing furnishings and equipment.

CARD DECK
A set of punched cards for data processing.

CARREL
(1) A small cubicle or study desk set aside for the use of learners or staff for individual study.
(2) A study station with unitized desk, table, or booth designed to facilitate individual study. A "wet carrel" includes electrical devices for use of instructional materials; a "dry carrel" lacks such devices.

CARTRIDGE
The case or container containing motion picture film, microfilm, and audio or videotape in an endless loop format.

CASSETTE
A case or container containing motion picture film, microfilm, and audio or videotape in a reel-to-reel format.

CATALOG
A list (any format) which records and describes the resources of a library. In a card catalog, unit entries are on separate cards, which are arranged in a definite order in drawers.

CATALOGED MATERIAL
Any library material which has been identified in a catalog which records, describes, and indexes the resources of a library; as distinct from a library's materials which

are merely physically arranged for use and are not in-
dexed and described individually by item.

CATHODE RAY STORAGE
An electrostatic storage device that utilizes a cathode
ray beam for access to the data.

CATHODE RAY TUBE (CRT)
A television-type tube used as a computer output for
graphics.

CENSUS
An enumeration or count of an entire population. See
Universe.

CENTRAL LIBRARY
The library which is the administrative center of a library system, often where the principal collections are
kept and handled. (Also called main library.)

CENTRAL PROCESSING UNIT (CPU)
A unit of a computer that includes the circuits control-
ling the interpretation and execution of instructions.
Synonymous with main frame.

CENTRALIZED PROCESSING
The ordering of library materials, preparation of catalog
records, and physical preparation in one library or a
central agency for all libraries of a system (or area).

CERTIFIED LIBRARIAN
A professional staff member who has been endorsed of-
ficially as having met the requirements for employment
set by a given state or governmental unit.

CHANNEL
(1) A specific band of frequencies assigned to each radio
    or television station. In some closed-circuit instal-
    lations, the video and audio signals are fed into an
    audio mixer tuned to a specific channel, enabling the
    signals to travel by means of a coaxial-cable system.
(2) One of the parallel tracks on computer tape used for
    storage of data.

CHARACTER SET
A systemized group of characters, such as the English
alphabet.

CHARACTERS PER INCH
A measure of character density on computer tapes. See also Density.

CHART
An opaque sheet exhibiting information in graphic or tabular form, or by use of contours, shapes, or figures.

CHILDREN'S DEPARTMENT
The administrative unit of a library system that has charge of work with children in a central children's room and in all other agencies offering library service to children.

CIRCULATION
The activity of a library in lending its resources to borrowers. For statistical purposes, photocopies or recordings provided in lieu of circulation should also be included.

CLASSIFICATION
(1) A systematic scheme for the arrangement of library materials according to subject or form.
(2) The assigning of library materials to their proper places in a system of classification.
(3) In archives administration, the arrangement in logical order of the series or files within a record group or of the record groups within an archival collection.

CLAW
The pull-down mechanism on a movie camera or projector which pulls down one frame of film at a time while a shutter covers the movement.

CLERICAL PERSONNEL
Staff members performing activities concerned with preparing, transferring, transcribing, systematizing, or filing written communications and records. Included are stenographers and secretaries.

CLIENTELE
The persons actually using the library's services. (Also known as library users or patrons.)

CLIPPING
An item of publication cut out of a newspaper, periodical or other printed document.

CODE
   (1) A set of unambiguous rules specifying the way in which
       data may be represented, e. g. , the set of corres-
       pondence in the standard code for information inter-
       exchange. Synonymous with coding scheme.
   (2) In telecommunications, a system of rules and conven-
       tions according to which the signals representing data
       can be formed, transmitted, received and processed.
   (3) In data processing, to represent data or a computer
       program in symbolic form that can be accepted by a
       data processor.

CODEN
   A five-character, alphanumeric code that provides concise, unique, and unambiguous identification of serial
   (all alphabetic characters) and non-serial (alphameric
   characters) titles. An alphameric check digit may be
   added as a sixth character to permit computer verifica-
   tion of the preceding five characters. The CODEN should
   be recorded in the format, "CODEN: CCCCCX. " CODEN
   assignment is controlled by a CODEN assignment center
   located at the Chemical Abstracts Service, Columbus,
   Ohio.

COLLATION
   The physical description of a work which guides the user
   in the selection of any equipment which may be necessary
   to utilize the material.

COLLECTION
   The total resources of organized materials provided by
   a library or media center for its clientele. (Also called
   resources or holdings.)

COMMUNITY ANTENNA RELAY SYSTEM (CARS)
   An FCC-authorized microwave frequency band for relay-
   ing television signals to cable television systems.

COMMUNITY SERVICES
   Special services provided by a library for the community as a whole or for some segment of the community,
   e. g. , lectures, concerts, book or art exhibits, discussion programs, and story hours.

COMPILATIONS
   Data presentations which are constructed from existing
   tabulations. If a user's needs may be met by reorganiz-

ing existing tabulations or calculating measures from
existing tabulations, the work is termed a compilation.

COMPUTER
An electronic data processor that can perform substan-
tial computation, including numerous arithmetic or logic
operations without intervention by a human operator during
the run.

COMPUTER CARD
A standard card designed to be punched with a pattern of
machine-readable holes representing data. (Also called
a Data Card.)

COMPUTER CENTER
An area which houses a computer, with spaces for the
computer itself and for peripheral devices for capturing,
manipulating and presentation of data and tape drives.
The area may also include space for staff and storage
of computer-related materials.

COMPUTER CONSOLE
That part of a computer used for communication between
the operator or maintenance engineer and the computer.

COMPUTER GRAPHICS
Techniques for graphically displaying data using a computer and associated output devices such as a printer,
pen plotter, or cathode ray tube. Through the use of
computer graphics, large amounts of data can be easily
visualized or displayed.

COMPUTER MAGNETIC TAPE
The magnetic tape designed for computer use and upon
which machine-readable data for computer can be recorded.

COMPUTER NETWORK
A complex consisting of two or more interconnected computers.

COMPUTER-OUTPUT MICROFILM (COM)
Microfilm containing data produced by a recorder from
computer-generated electrical signals.

COMPUTER-OUTPUT MICROFILMER
A recorder which converts data from a computer into
human-readable language and records it onto microfilm.

COMPUTER PRINTOUT
The printed output of a computer, usually on a continuous sheet of paper. Specifically designed forms for printing information with a computer printer are also recorded here.

COMPUTER PROGRAM
A series of instructions or statements, in a form acceptable to a computer, prepared in order to achieve a certain result.

COMPUTER TERMINAL
A unit which permits one or two-way communication between a user and a computer via communications lines. The device may include features such as a cathode ray tube, typewriter/teletype unit, light pen, printer, plasma panel, television receiver, touch sensitive panel, keyboard, card reader, tape reader or audio output unit.

CONSOLIDATED SYSTEM
A public library system established by vote of several local governing bodies or by action of voters, and governed by the board of trustees of the system, with individual units operating as branches of the system.

CONSORTIUM   See   Library Consortium

CONSULTATIVE SERVICES   See   Advisory Services

CONTRACT SERVICES
Items appearing in a library's statement of income representing funds received from a governmental, library, or other agency for specific services rendered, or in the statement of expenditures for services rendered to the library by individuals or agencies on the basis of a specific contract.

CONTRIBUTED SERVICES
Services in lieu of compensation, the cost of which is a part of normal overhead costs and the value of which can be estimated.

CONVERSION DATA
The process of changing information from one physical form or representation to another, such as from the bit arrangements required by one type of computer to that required by another.

COOPERATIVE SERVICES
The common services planned and coordinated by a cooperative system.

COOPERATIVE SYSTEM See Library Consortium

CORRESPONDENCE INSTRUCTION
Instruction which is dependent on the systematic exchange between teacher and learner(s) of materials sent by mail.

COST BENEFIT
Analysis which provides the means for comparing the resources to be allocated to a specific program with results likely to be obtained from it; or analysis which provides the means for comparing the results likely to be obtained from the allocation of certain resources toward the achievement of alternate or competing objectives.

COST EFFECTIVENESS
Analysis designed to measure the extent to which resources allocated to a specific objective under each of several alternatives actually contribute to accomplishing the objective, so that different ways of gaining the objective may be compared.

COUNTY LIBRARY
A free public library service to county residents supported with county tax funds and administered as an independent agency or as part of another library agency.

CPU See Central Processing Unit

CREATOR
The author, composer, photographer or other person(s) responsible for the intellectual or artistic content of a work.

CREATOR MAIN ENTRY
The basic entry in the catalog for which the heading is the name of the creator of a work.

CREDITS
Information placed at the beginning or end of many film formats, giving names of the cast, technicians, distributor and other pertinent data.

CROSS-TABULATIONS
Tabulations of data structured by other data characteristics. For example, years of age by sex and race.

DATA
A general term used to denote any or all facts or quantities represented by numbers, letters, or symbols.
The term also denotes basic elements of information
that can be processed or produced by a computer.

DATA BANK
A comprehensive collection of libraries of data. For
example, one line of an invoice may form an item, a
complete invoice may form a record, a complete set
of such records may form a file, the collection of in-
ventory control files may form a library, and the libraries used by an organization are known as its data
bank.

DATA BASE   See   Data Bank

DATA ITEM
A cell of data appearing in a tabulation; sometimes referred to as a tally cell. One of the numbers appearing in a table.

DATA PROCESSING
The execution of a systematic sequence of operations
performed upon data.

DATA PROCESSOR
A device capable of performing data processing, including desk calculators, punched card machines, and
computers. Synonymous with processor.

DENSITY
The number of characters or groups of bits recorded on
an inch of tape. Frequently used densities are 556,
800, or 1600 cpi (characters per inch). A particular
computer system is capable of reading only certain
specified densities of magnetic tape.

DEPARTMENT
(1) A major administrative unit of a library system set
up to perform a definite function or set of related
functions, and having its own staff and specified
responsibilities, with a head directly responsible to
the library director or to the assistant director.

(2) A subject section in a library in which all books, periodicals, and other library materials, whether for reference or circulation, are separated according to subject into several divisions (as in some large public libraries); sometimes called division.

DEPARTMENT/DIVISION HEAD
The head of a library or library system or a section devoted to a particular subject or group of subjects.

DEPARTMENTAL LIBRARY
In colleges and universities, a special area or subject collection of library materials, possibly housed within the main library, and administratively linked to the branches. For a library maintained by a government department, See Government Library.

DEPOSIT COLLECTION
A number of films, records, or tapes loaned, without cost, from a central source to a given library or system which had the responsibility for their circulation and maintenance. Normally, the collection must be returned to the source at a specified date. The collection does not go on to another library or system. The costs to the library served are limited to inspection, maintenance, and postage. Deposit collections are beginning to be used now with other audiovisual formats. Not to be confused with Bicycling or Film Circuits.

DEPOSIT STATION
A public library agency in a store, school, factory, club, or other organization or institution, with a small and frequently changed collection of books, and open at certain designated times. (Also called station.)

DEPOSITORY LIBRARY See Documents Depository

DIGITAL COMPUTER
(1) A computer in which discrete representation of data is mainly used.
(2) A computer that operates on discrete data by performing arithmetic and logic processes on these data.

DIORAMA
A three-dimensional representation of a scene.

DIRECT ACCESS (ADP)
(1) Pertaining to the process of obtaining data from or

placing data into storage where the time required for such access is independent of the location of the data most recently obtained or placed in storage.

(2) Pertaining to a storage device such as a drama or disk in which the access time is effectively independent of the location of the data.

DIRECTORY
(1) (ADP): An index to the location of the variable fields (control and data) within a bibliographic record. The directory consists of entries.

(2) Library: A reference work designed to give the name and address, the size of collection(s), subjects, staff, geographic area (national, regional, local) covered, and type (public, college, university, research, or school library, information or documentation center).

DISCARD
To withdraw a book, periodical volume, film, recording, or other item from the collection and from any records. See also Weeding.

DISCOGRAPHY
A list of recordings on a specific subject or area of information. See also Bibliography.

DISSOLVE
The fading out of one scene in a film and its replacement with another scene fading in. Used to indicate a change of setting or a lapse of time.

DISTRIBUTOR
Company from which materials may be purchased, rented, or borrowed. Most often used to denote the agency which has acquired legal rights of distribution from the producer or copyright proprietor.

DOCUMENT
(1) A medium and the data recorded on it for human use, e. g. , a report sheet, a book.

(2) By extension, any record that has permanence and that can be read by man or machine.

DOCUMENTARY
A factual film, shot with real people in actual settings. (National Geographic and Jacques Cousteau programs are popular examples.)

DOCUMENTS DEPOSITORY
A library legally designated to receive without charge
copies of all or selected U. S. Government publications.

DOLBY SYSTEM
An electronic method which reduces noise in audio recordings.

DUMP (ADP)
A printout of the contents of a computer tape, disk, or
core storage.

EDITION
The entire number of copies of a work produced from
the same master and issued at one time or at intervals.

EDUCATIONAL LEVEL
The level of understanding or educational attainment for
which a work is intended.

EDUCATIONAL MEDIA
The equipment and materials used for communication in
instruction.   Includes motion pictures, television, printed
materials, computer-based instruction, graphic and
photographic materials, sound recordings, and three-
dimensional objects.

EDUCATIONAL RESOURCE INFORMATION CENTER (ERIC)
Data banks on microfilm of documents relating to education.

EDUCATIONAL TECHNOLOGY
The broad application of scientific processes to the solu-
tion of educational problems.

EDUCATIONAL TOY
A play item which has value in developing physical or
mental capacities and manipulative and motor skills, in
addition to its value for pleasure and recreation.

EFLA
The Educational Film Library Association, the nation's
largest clearinghouse for nontheatrical film information,
founded in 1943.   It sponsors the annual American Film
Festival.

EIAJ-1
Electronics Industries Association of Japan Standard for

$\frac{1}{2}$-inch videotape reel recordings. Also called Japan
Type 1 Standard.

ELECTRONIC DATA PROCESSING (EDP) See Automatic
Data Processing

EPHEMERA
Material of transitory interest or value, consisting generally of pamphlets or clippings, which are usually kept
for a limited time in vertical files.

EQUIPMENT
Items of a nonexpendable nature which retain their basic
identity and utility over a period of time, as contrasted
with supplies.

EXHIBIT
A collection of objects and materials arranged in a setting to convey a unified idea.

FEATURE FILM
A film made for commercial theater distribution, usually
in the 35mm or 70mm format (example: King Kong).

FEDERATED SYSTEM
A library system formed by action of governing bodies
in which existing libraries continue to be governed by
local boards; the central administration of the federated
system coordinates and advises on cooperative services.

FILE
(1) Any equipment, such as vertical file, visible file,
    etc. , in which records, cards, pamphlets, clippings,
    etc. , are kept.
(2) A collection of materials such as cards, pamphlets,
    clippings, etc. , arranged systematically for reference.

FILE MAINTENANCE
The periodic updating of a file, by adding, changing or
deleting records.

FILM CIRCUIT
A group of libraries which has formed an organization
to circulate motion picture film on a rotating basis to
each member library. Groups of film remain at each
member library for a stated period of time, and inspection is done on a regular basis.

FILMLOOP
   Film spliced in a loop for continuous playing without rewinding.

FILMSLIP
   A short filmstrip, usually in rigid format or a rigid
   holder and without sound accompaniment.

FILMSTRIP
   A length of film that presents a sequence of related still
   pictures for projection one at a time. Most filmstrips
   are on 35mm film but some are 16mm or smaller. A
   filmstrip is single-frame if the horizontal axis of the
   pictures is perpendicular to the sprocket holes; it is
   double-frame if the horizontal axis of the pictures is
   parallel to the sprocket holes. It may or may not have
   provision for sound accompaniment. (Also called Strip-
   film.)

FILMSTRIP PROJECTOR
   A device designed to project filmstrips (usually 35mm)
   and which normally projects a single-frame filmstrip
   and may project a double-frame filmstrip.

FILMSTRIP, SILENT
   A filmstrip without an accompanying audiorecording. A
   silent filmstrip is usually accompanied by a script or
   has captions printed on the frames.

FILMSTRIP/SLIDE PROJECTOR
   A filmstrip projector (usually silent) equipped with an
   adapter or carrier to accept 2-by-2-inch slides.

FILMSTRIP, SOUND
   A filmstrip accompanied by a separate audiorecording,
   which may also have a signal for the filmstrip to be
   advanced as well as a sound track related to the filmstrip.

FILMSTRIP VIEWER
   A device equipped with a built-in viewing glass or rear
   projection screen for viewing filmstrips, usually single-
   frame filmstrips.

FISCAL PERIOD
   A designated period at the end of which a library or
   library system determines its financial condition and the

results of its operations, and closes its books. The
period is usually a year, though not necessarily a calendar year.

FLIC
The Film Library Information Council, an organization
for public library film librarians.

FOUR-CHANNEL SOUND
Sound reproduction with four discrete output signals
(usually with two speakers in front and two speakers in
back of the listener) to achieve a three-dimensional
effect. Also used to denote any related recordings,
equipment, and techniques.

FRAMING
Moving the film gate aperture so that the frame of a
film is correctly centered on the screen.

FREQUENCY MODULATION (FM)
A system of static-free radio transmission based on the
reversal of the usual system (amplitude modulation) in
that the power output remains constant while the frequency of the waves is varied.

GAME
A set of materials developed to be used according to
prescribed rules for (physical or mental) competitive
play.

GENERAL COLLECTION
That part of a library's holdings containing basic materials as distinct from special collections.

GIFT AND EXCHANGE
The acquisition of library materials by gift, or in exchange with another institution for publications of that
institution.

GLOBE
A sphere upon which is depicted a map of the earth or
the heavens, showing elements in their relationships.

GOVERNMENT DOCUMENT
Any printed publication or microfilm bearing a government imprint, e. g. , the publication of federal, state,
local, or foreign governments; and of world organiza-

tions, such as United Nations, European Common Market, etc.

GRANT
An item of library income deriving from state or federal funds or other source, or an item of state or federal expenditure for subsidies to libraries.

GRAPHIC MATERIALS
Instructional materials conveying meaning largely through line representations or symbols that are nearer to reality than verbal symbols. Examples are maps, charts, diagrams, poster, cartoons, and graphs. (Also called Graphics.)

HARD COPY
A printed copy of machine output in an eye-readable form; for example, printed reports, listings, and documents.

HARDWARE
(1) Physical equipment, as opposed to the computer program or method of use; e. g., mechanical, magnetic, electrical, or electronic devices. Contrast with software.
(2) Equipment for the use of audiovisual and microform materials.

HOLOGRAM
A three-dimensional image usually produced by laser photography.

HOURS OF SERVICE
Those hours during the week when a library is open and prepared to render service to its clientele.

IMPRINT
The area of the catalog entry which records information about the production or publication of a work. The elements in the imprint are place, producer, or publisher/ sponsor/distributor.

INAUDIBLE SIGNAL
The inaudible pulse on audiorecordings designed to accompany synchronized filmstrips and slide sets. The pulse activates the mechanism which advances the material through the projector.

INFORMATION CENTER
An organizational unit established for the purpose of acquiring, selecting, storing, retrieving, evaluating, analyzing and disseminating a body of information. When an
information center is in a specialized field or pertains
to a specified mission, the emphasis is on analyzing,
synthesizing, and repackaging.

INFORMATION CLEARINGHOUSE
A type of special library which has a limited amount of
published material on file, but gathers and relays information by telephone and correspondence and by the
use of other libraries.

INFORMATION NETWORK
A cooperative system established by libraries and information centers which are brought together by a common
subject to share informational resources, human resources, equipment, technology and all other elements
essential for providing effective information services.

INFORMATION RETRIEVAL
The methods and procedures for recovering specific information from stored data.

INSERVICE TRAINING
Informal education in librarianship taken by a staff member or student librarian, often consisting of institutes or
workshops. Such education usually does not entail college credit but may fulfill certain requirements for cer-
tificates. Also called on-the-job training.

INSTITUTIONAL LIBRARY
A library maintained by a public or private institution,
such as a prison library or a hospital library.

INSTRUCTION
The process of creating or making available experiences
which facilitate learning.

INSTRUCTIONAL DEVELOPMENT
The application of research concerning learner, learning
task, and presentation variables to the design and production of instructional products and the evaluation of
these products according to prespecified criteria.

INSTRUCTIONAL LEVEL
An indication of the general nature and difficulty of in-

struction, e. g. , elementary instructional level, secondary instructional level, and postsecondary instructional level.

INSTRUCTIONAL PRODUCT
Any material or group of materials produced for instructional purposes; use of this term in educational technology is limited to items that are replicable and reproducible.

INSTRUCTIONAL SYSTEM
An integrated group of program components organized to accomplish specified instructional objectives.

INSTRUCTIONAL TECHNOLOGY
That part of educational technology concerned with applying scientific processes to teaching and learning activities.

INTERLIBRARY COOPERATION
(1) Cooperation among two or more libraries of any type, including but not limited to participation in networks and consortia.
(2) For purposes of the administration of the Library Services and Construction Act, this term means the establishment, expansion and operation of local, regional, and interstate cooperative library networks which will provide for the systematic and effective coordination of the resources of school, public, academic and special libraries and information centers for improved supplementary services for the special clientele served by each type of library or center. Such networks may be designed to serve a community, metropolitan area, or region within a state, or may serve a statewide or multistate area and shall consist of two or more types of libraries.

INTERLIBRARY LOAN
Transactions in which one library makes its library materials available to another library for their use by an individual.   They include the provision of copies as substitutes for loans of the original materials.

INTERLIBRARY LOAN CODE
The National Interlibrary Loan Code adopted by the Reference Services Division acting for the American Library Association on June 27, 1968 governs the interlibrary lending relations among libraries on the national level, among research libraries, and among libraries not operating under special or local codes.

INTERLIBRARY REFERENCE SERVICE
A cooperative arrangement among libraries whereby
reference work is done by one library for a patron of
another library which is not an integral part of the same
system.

INTERNATIONAL STANDARD BIBLIOGRAPHIC DESCRIPTION -
Monographs (ISBD) (M)
A punctuation scheme designed to facilitate the computer-
ization of bibliographic data.

INTERNATIONAL STANDARD BOOK NUMBER (ISBN)
A four-part, ten-character code that provides a unique,
title identification of a specific non-serial publication issued by particular publisher. The four parts of the ISBN
are: group identifier (e. g., national, geographic, language, or other convenient group); publisher identifier;
title identifier; check digit. The ISBN is in the general
form of ISBN X-XXXX-XXXX-C, where the first three
groups may vary in length. ISBN assignment is controlled by the International Standard Book Numbering
Agency.

INTERNATIONAL STANDARD SERIAL NUMBER (ISSN)
The international numerical code identifies serial publications based on the American National Standard Identification Number for Serial Publications Z39. 9-1971 and
approved by International Standards Organization Technical Committee 46.

ISSN   See   International Standard Serial Number

KINESCOPE
A motion picture photographed from a television screen.

KIT
A collection of materials in more than one medium that
is subject-related and intended for use as an instructional unit. Does not include sound filmstrips, slide/audio-
tapes, and similar items unless they are accompanied by
other materials.

LANGUAGE LABORATORY
A space specially designed, adapted, and/or designated
for the teaching of languages, usually modern spoken
languages. Such space may have tape recorders, individual carrels, listening stations, and other materials

and equipment to facilitate the audiolingual method of
language teaching.

LANTERN SLIDE
An image, glass-mounted, on film or other transparent
material, $3\frac{1}{4}$ x 4 inches (8 x 10 cm.), intended for projection.

LANTERN SLIDE PROJECTOR
A slide projector designed to accept standard $3\frac{1}{4}$ x 4-inch
lantern slides, and occasionally smaller slides with the
provision of special adapters and, usually, a different
projection lens.

LEADER
A length of film used to thread the projector so none of
the actual picture is lost or damaged in threading.

LEARNING
Simply defined, learning is a change in behavior (usually
relatively permanent) acquired by an organism as a result of practice or experience. The actual internal process of learning is generally inferred rather than directly
observed. Learning does not include behavior changes
as a result of general or natural conditions such as physical development, although such factors do play a part
in learning. In instruction, the term learning usually
connotes conscious attempts of the learner to acquire
cognitive and psychomotor skills. Learning and instruction are two sides of the same coin; the former is the
acquisition of new behaviors (whether cognitive, affective,
or psychomotor) and the latter is the planning and implementation of these experiences through which the learner
will acquire the desired behaviors.

LIBRARIAN
(1) The head of a library, library system, or school library. Also known as chief librarian, or library
director.
(2) A professional member of a library staff.
(3) Combined with name of department or type of work,
the term is used to designate the title of a staff
member (e.g., children's librarian, school librarian,
etc.).

LIBRARY
Irrespective of its title, any organized collection of

printed books and periodicals or of any other graphic or
audiovisual materials, and the service of a staff to provide and facilitate the use of such materials as are required to meet the informational, research, educational,
or recreational needs of its users; also its physical facilities.

LIBRARY CONSORTIUM
A formal arrangement of two or more libraries not under
the same institutional control for joint activities to improve the library service of the participants by cooperation extending beyond traditional interlibrary loan.

LIBRARY DISTRICT
(1) An area designated for subsidies, system activities,
or other administrative purposes.
(2) An area in which the citizens have voted to assume
a tax to support a library.

LIBRARY GENERAL INFORMATION SURVEY (LIBGIS)
A program of the National Center for Education Statistics of the U. S. Department of Health, Education, and
Welfare initiated in 1974 for periodic national surveys
of the principal types of libraries in the United States
in cooperation with state library and education agencies.

LIBRARY OF CONGRESS CLASSIFICATION
A system of classification for books developed by the
Library of Congress for its collections. It has a no-
tation of letters and figures that allows for expansion.

LIBRARY MATERIALS
Those print and nonprint items provided by the library
for its clientele. This does not include equipment with
which to see, near, or read the items (e. g. , projectors,
phonographs, readers).

LIBRARY SCHOOL
A professional school, department, or division granting
a post-baccalaureate degree, and organized and maintained by an institution of higher education for the purpose of preparing students for entrance into the library
profession.

LIBRARY SYSTEM
(1) An organization with a common administration in
which independent library units share services and
resources.

(2) A central library and all of its other service outlets, i. e. , branches, deposit stations, bookmobiles.

LIBRARY TECHNICIAN
A person with certain specifically library-related skills-- in preliminary bibliographic searching, for example, or utilization of certain equipment.

LISTENING CENTER
An audio distribution device into which headsets can be connected to enable more than one learner to listen to an audio program.   It may have more than one channel and may have volume controls.   The entire unit may be permanently mounted or packed into a storage case.

LOOP
A short length of film, audiotape, or videotape, with its ends joined together in a continuous loop to provide play-back without rewinding.

MACHINE-READABLE CATALOGING (MARC)
A program developed initially by the Library of Congress for placing machine-readable cataloging information in a standard format on computer tape.

MACHINE-READABLE DATA FILE (ADP)
A collection of related records that are treated as a unit and presented in such a way that they can be used and/ or translated by machine.

MAGNETIC TAPE (ADP)
A film that has one of its sides coated with iron or other oxide that can be magnetized.   It is used as both an in-put and output medium with computers, audio and video recordings, etc.

MAIN ENTRY
The basic catalog entry giving all the information neces-sary for the complete identification of a work.

MANUSCRIPT
The handwritten or typewritten copy of an author's work before it is printed.

MAP
A representation, usually on a flat surface, of the earth or the heavens.   Navigational charts are included in this category.

MARC SERVICE
A subscription service of the Library of Congress for
providing (MARC) tapes to libraries and other users.

MEASURE (noun)
A unit of measurement to which reference may be made
for purposes of description, comparison, and evaluation.
Many measures are obtained by computation involving
one or more items of information.

MEDIA CENTER
An area or system of areas in a school or library where
a full range of information sources, associated equipment, and services from media staff are accessible.

MEDIA CODE
An alpha code designed to facilitate the storage and retrieval of bibliographic and statistical records.

MEDIA SPECIALIST
A staff member whose activities require professional
training and skill in educational media and its utilization
in education.

MEDIA TECHNICIAN
A media staff member with skills in such fields as
graphics production and display, information and materials processing, photographic production, operating and
maintenance of audiovisual equipment and/or television
equipment, and in the technical and/or installation of
systems components.

MEDIAGRAPHY   See   Bibliography for definition

MEDIAMOBILE
A truck or van specially designed and operated to distribute print and audiovisual materials; serves both as
a delivery unit and a branch or satellite library.   See
also Bookmobile.

MEDIUM DESIGNATOR
The term which identifies the basic or general physical
format of a work.

MICROFICHE
A sheet of microfilm containing multiple microimages
in a grid pattern.   It usually contains a title which can
be read without magnification.   See also Ultramicrofiche.

MICROFILM
A fine-grain, high resolution film containing an image
greatly reduced in size from the original.

MICROFILM CARD
A general term for camera cards, copy cards, image
cards and aperture cards.

MICROFORM
Any material, film or paper, printed or photographic,
containing microimages which are units of information,
such as a page of text or drawing, too small to be read
without magnification.

MICROPRINT
Microimages on opaque stock, produced by printing as
distinct from microimages produced on a photosensitive
material.

MICROPROJECTOR
A device designed to enlarge and project microscopic
transparencies such as microscope slides or sections of
microfilms for viewing by large audiences.

MODEL
A three-dimensional representation of a real thing, produced in the exact size of the original, or on a smaller
or larger scale.   Includes sculptural reproduction.

MONOGRAPH
A systematic and complete treatise on a particular subject, usually detached in treatment.   It is generally a
book or pamphlet, but need not be bibliographically independent.

MONOPHONIC
Sound reproduction with a single output signal.   Also
used to denote any related recordings, equipment, and
techniques.

MOTION PICTURE FILM
A flexible, usually transparent material, with or without a magnetic or optical sound track, bearing a sequence of images which create the illusion of movement
when projected in rapid succession (usually 18 or 24
frames per second).   Common film sizes in public library use are 16mm, 8mm, and super 8mm.

MOTION PICTURE PROJECTOR
A device designed to project motion pictures. It may be
equipped to reproduce sound on either magnetic, optical,
or both types of sound tracks and may have audio recording capability. The most common types of motion
picture projectors in instructional institutions are 16mm,
8mm, and super 8mm.

MULTI-MEDIA KIT See Kit

NETWORK, LIBRARY
Formal organization among libraries for cooperating and
sharing of resources, usually with an explicitly hierarch-
ical structure, in which the group as a whole is organized into subgroups with the expectation that most of the
needs of a library will be satisfied within the subgroup
of which it is a member.

NONPRINT MATERIALS
Materials which involve media other than the print medium (e.g., pictures, images, graphics, etc.). Many
graphic materials are actually printed, but the term nonprint has come to mean those materials which are not
textual or book-like in nature. The terms media, nonprint, and nonbook are often used interchangeably.

OCR See Optical Character Recognition

OFFLINE (ADP)
The equipment or devices not under control of the central computer processing unit.

ONLINE (ADP)
The equipment or devices under control of the central
computer processing unit.

OPAQUE PROJECTOR
A device designed to project images of nontransparent,
flat objects, such as maps, pictures, or printed pages,
onto a screen by using light reflected from the opaque
object. The maximum original image size is usually
10 x 10 inches.

OPERATING EXPENDITURES
Those costs necessary to the rendering of library service, i.e., expenditures for personnel, library materials, binding and supplies, repair or replacement of

existing furnishings and equipment, and usually costs
necessary for the maintenance of plant.

OPTICAL CHARACTER RECOGNITION (OCR)
The machine identification of printed characters through
use of light-sensitive devices.   Contrast with magnetic
ink character recognition.

ORIGINAL CATALOGING
A determination of the descriptive material to be contained in the bibliographic record, from the physical
item.

OVERHEAD PROJECTOR
A device designed to project images from transparent
and translucent materials.   The projector is placed in
front of the viewers and may be used in a semidarkened
or completely lighted room.   Models are available for
accepting transparencies from $3\frac{1}{4}$ x 4 inches to 10 x 10
inches.

OVERHEAD TRANSPARENCY
An image on a transparent sheet or material up to 10"
by 10" intended for use with an overhead projector or
light box.

PARAPROFESSIONAL
A skilled, specially trained, nonprofessional assistant
who performs essential tasks under the direction of a
professional, freeing the professional to devote more of
his/her time to strictly professional responsibilities.
It is often used as a term which is equivalent to technician.   See also Professional.

PATENT
An official document issued by a national government,
securing to an inventor the exclusive ɪɪgnɪ to make,
use, and vend his invention for a term of years.

PERFORMANCE STANDARDS
The absolute or comparative levels of behavior required
to determine achievement of specified objectives.

PERIPHERAL EQUIPMENT (ADP)
In a data processing system, any unit of equipment,
distinct from the central processing unit, which may
provide the system with outside communication.

PERSONNEL COSTS
A category of library expenditures comprising items relating to the staffing of the library, except those for which the library contracts with an outside party; e. g., salaries and wages before any deductions for Social Security, hospitalization, retirement. Includes fringe benefits. See also Fringe Benefits.

PHOTOGRAPH
An image produced on a sensitized surface by the action of light.

PICTURE
A representation made on opaque material by drawing, painting, photography, or other graphic arts techniques.

POPULATION SERVED
The number of persons making up a municipality, industrial or governmental establishment, academic community, organization, etc. to which the activities of an individual library are directed; as distinguished from clientele, which represents the number of persons actually using that library's services.

POSTER
A large illustration designed for display.

PRECATALOGED MATERIAL
An item which is accompanied by catalog cards obtained through purchase, contract, or agreement from a commercial concern or library. See also Preprocessed Material.

PREPROCESSED MATERIAL
Items which have been physically prepared for use by a commercial concern or other agencies and obtained through purchase, contract, or agreement. Such physical preparation may include jacketing, pocketing, stamping, etc. See also Precataloged Material.

PREVIEW PRINT
A film, filmstrip, or videotape customarily loaned without charge to a library by the producer or distributor to evaluate for possible purchase. It is similar to the publishing practice of sending approval copies of books to selected librarians.

PREVIEWING
The act of screening a preview print, tape or other work. In the library itself it refers to a service to patrons whereby the library allows them to prescreen an item in order to select appropriate material for a program.

PRICE INDEXES FOR LIBRARY MATERIALS
Price indexes to measure yearly changes in the average list prices of certain library materials were developed and promulgated as Criteria for Price Indexes for Library Materials, an American Standard (Z39.20-1974). These price indexes currently cover only hardcover, trade, and technical books; paperback books; periodicals; serial services; and rates for library-produced microfilm.

PRINT
All 16mm and 8mm films in libraries are prints. If a library has three copies of a film, for example, it is counted as three prints but is listed as one title. Film holdings are usually listed as so many titles and so many prints or items.

PRINTOUT (ADP)
A paper copy of data records reported from the computer system through a printing device.

PROFESSIONAL
A person who has had extensive training in a particular area and who performs tasks which require a high degree of problem solving, data analysis and synthesis. Tasks tend to be specified in terms of a general problem to be solved.

PROFESSIONAL STAFF OTHER THAN LIBRARIANS AND
MEDIA SPECIALISTS
Persons who, though not librarians and media specialists, are in positions normally requiring at least a bachelor's degree (e.g., curators, archivists, computer specialists, information and system specialists, subject bibliographers, subject specialists).

PROGRAM (ADP)
The complete set of instructions which determine the sequence and type of computer actions.

PROGRAMMED INSTRUCTION KIT
A sequential presentation of material on a given subject

designed to lead the user step-by-step to an understanding of the subject.

PUBLIC LIBRARY
    A library that serves free all residents of a given com-
    munity, district, or region, and receives its financial
    support, in whole or in part, from public funds. In ad-
    dition to the tax-supported municipal, county, and re-
    gional public libraries, this definition includes privately
    controlled libraries which render, without charge, gen-
    eral library service to the community.

PUBLIC SCHOOL
    A school operated by publicly elected or appointed school
    officials in which the program and activities are under
    the control of these officials and which is supported pri-
    marily by public funds.

PUBLIC (SERVICE) AREA
    That portion of the reader area allocated to public ser-
    vice desks (such as circulation desk, information desk,
    registration desk), the card catalog, and exhibits and
    displays.

PUZZLE
    A work which presents a problem that requires solution
    and tests problem-solving skills.

READY REFERENCE
    Reference service involving questions of a factual nature
    which can be answered readily, and often for which a
    special collection of standard reference tools is developed,
    as distinguished from literature searches.

REALIA
    Tangible objects, real items (as opposed to representa-
    tions or models) as they are without alterations.

RECORD PLAYER
    A device with built-in amplifier and speakers which re-
    produces sound from audiodiscs. Also called audiodisc
    player or phonograph.

REFERENCE DEPARTMENT
    The administrative unit or units in charge of the refer-
    ence work of a library.

REFERENCE QUESTION
Any request for information which requires the use
of one or more sources to determine the answer and
utilizes the professional judgment of a librarian.

REPORT
An official or formal record, as of some special investi-
gation of the activities of a corporate body, etc.

RESERVATION
Locating the holding material for a patron. It may include some sort of notification procedure by the library,
but the responsibility for obtaining, transporting, and
returning the material is usually the patron's.

RESERVE COLLECTION
Materials which have been removed from the general
circulating collection and set aside in a library or media center so that they will be on hand for special purposes. Usually the circulation and length of loan of
items in a reserve collection are restricted so that they
will be available to those who have need of them within
a limited time period.

RIIA
The Record Industry Association of America, which sets
recording standards for the industry.

SALARY RANGE
The lowest and the highest salaries actually paid to in-
cumbents of a given position classification.

SALARIES AND WAGES
In library statistical surveys, expenditures for salaries
and wages before any deductions and excluding "fringe
benefits. "

SCORE
The written or printed form of a musical work in which
the music for the participating voices and or instruments
appears on two or more staves one above the other.

SCREEN
A prepared surface on which images are projected.
Screens may be portable or fixed installation, front or
rear projection.

SCULPTURE
   A three-dimensional artwork.

SEQUENCE
   The order of presentation of aspects of the instructional
   program, as within a grade, a course, or a series of
   grades or courses.

SERIAL
   A publication issued in successive parts, usually at regular intervals, and as a rule, intended to be continued
   indefinitely. Serials include newspapers, periodicals,
   annuals (reports, yearbooks, etc.), memoirs, proceedings, and transactions of societies; they may include
   monographic and publishers' series.

SERIES
   A group of separate works, numbered or unnumbered,
   usually related to one another by subject or content and
   bearing a collective title.

SHARED CATALOGING
   A system for determining bibliographic descriptions for
   local holdings by utilizing the information provided by
   another library to catalog the item.

SHELF LIST
   A record of the items in a collection arranged in the
   order in which they are on the shelves.

SHELVING CAPACITY
   Number of linear feet of shelf space.

SLIDE
   A transparent image on film or glass (usually photographic) intended for use with a slide projector.

SLIDE PROJECTOR
   A device designed to project slides on transparencies
   mounted in small frames, usually 2" by 2". Some models have provision for sound and/or accept trays, cartridges, or drums.

SLIDE VIEWER
   A device equipped with a built-in viewing glass or rear
   projector screen for viewing slides. Models are available with provision for playing accompanying audiorecordings.

SOFTWARE
> A term which originated in the computer field to describe
> the programs and instructions required for directing the
> operation of a computer system. The term is popularly
> used in educational circles to refer to materials, such
> as filmstrips and films, which are used with equipment
> or hardware.

SOUND RECORDER
> A generic term for any of several devices which can re-
> cord sounds. The term includes audiotape recorders,
> wire recorders, magnetic film recorders, and is occa-
> sionally used to designate the audio or sound portion of
> a motion picture camera equipped for sound recordings.
> (Also called "audio recorder. ")

SPECIAL COLLECTION
> A collection within a library of material of a certain
> form, on a certain subject, of a certain period or geo-
> graphical area, or gathered for some particular reason.

SPECIAL LIBRARY
> One maintained by an association, government service,
> parliament, research institution, learned society, pro-
> fessional association, museum, business firm, industrial
> enterprise, chamber of commerce, or other organized
> group, the greater part of their collections being in a
> specific field or subject, e. g. , natural sciences, social
> sciences, agriculture, chemistry, medicine, economics,
> engineering, law, history.

SPECIMEN
> A part or sample which is typical of a group or object
> or is representative of a class.

STANDARDS
> Objective, observable, and usually quantitative measures
> of achievement set up as ideals of library service with
> which a particular library can be compared.

STEREOGRAPH
> A pair of opaque or transparent images (usually photo-
> graphic) intended to produce a three-dimensional effect
> when viewed with stereoscopic equipment.

STEREOPHONIC
> Sound reproduction with two separate, discrete output

signals. Also used to denote any related recordings,
equipment and techniques.

STORYBOARD
A series of sketches or pictures and any accompanying
text which visualize each topic or item in an audiovisual
medium to be produced.

STUDY PRINT
A picture generally with accompanying textual information
prepared specifically for instructional purposes.

SUPPLIES
Material items of an expendable nature that are con-
sumed, worn out, or deteriorate in use.

SYNCHRONIZATION (SYNC)
The matching of sound and image on a film or other
medium. When they are not matched, the item is said
to be "out of sync. "

SYSTEM
An organized assemblage of interrelated components designed to function as a whole to achieve predetermined
objectives.

SYSTEMS APPROACH
A rational procedure for designing a system for attaining specific objectives. The methodology includes, mi-
nimally, specification of objectives in measurable terms;
restatement of objectives in terms of capabilities and
constraints; development of possible approaches; selection
of appropriate approaches as a result of a trade-off
study; integration of the approaches; evaluation of the effectiveness of the system in attaining objectives.

TARGET AUDIENCE
That portion of the total population selected for exposure
to a specific program. This group is generally identified in terms of certain common social and/or learning
characteristics.

TECHNICIAN
A person with some specialized training who performs
tasks requiring the use of specified yet complex sequence
(or alternate sequences) of tasks, sometimes using

reference materials. Tasks tend to be assigned or described in terms of a specific, defined output, either
product or service.

TELECLASS
A method of teaching homebound individuals as a group;
the teacher uses an automatic dialer on the desk, and
buttons on the telephone console enable the teacher to
talk to the whole class of homebound individuals or to
each individual privately.

TELEVISION PROJECTOR
An electronic device that projects television images onto
a screen. Also called Television Beam Projector, Tele-
beam Projector.

TELEVISION RECEIVER
An electronic device which intercepts the signal of a
television broadcast or (with adaptation) television signals from other sources, amplifies and translates the
signals into image and sound.

TIME SHARING (ADP)
Multiple use of available computer time, often via ter-
minals.

TITLE
A publication which forms a separate bibliographic whole,
whether issued in one or several volumes, reels, discs,
slides, or parts. It applies equally to printed and to
non-printed materials, as books, periodicals, audiovisual
materials and microforms.

TITLE COUNT
Method for estimating the number of titles in a collection.

TRANSPARENCY See Overhead Transparency

ULTRAFICHE
Any microfiche with images reduced more than 90 times
of the original size. Not included in microfiche. (Also
called ultra microfiche.)

UNEXPENDED BALANCE
That portion of a library's current funds which is not
spent and not pledged toward a particular purpose, such
as a sinking fund. Unexpended funds may revert to the

appropriating unit or become part of the expendable funds
for the succeeding fiscal period.

UNIT COST
A term used in cost accounting to denote the cost of
producing a unit of product or rendering a unit of service, e. g. , the cost of cataloging a book.

UNIVERSE
In statistics, the totality of the group of items, persons,
or objects being surveyed. Also called a population.

UNIVERSE SURVEY
Collection of information from the entire universe or
population, as opposed to a sample survey.

VERTICAL FILE MATERIALS
Those items such as pamphlets, clippings, pictures, etc. ,
which, because of their shape and often their ephemeral
nature, are filed vertically in drawers for ready reference.

VIDEODISC, RECORDED
A disc on which are recorded video and/or audio signals
for television use. A videodisc requires a videoplayer
compatible with the videodisc.

VIDEOPLAYER
A device which can reproduce sound and pictures from a
videotape or videodisc on a television monitor or special
receiver. It cannot record images or sound. The unit
may use videotape on reels or in cartridges or cassettes.

VIDEOTAPE, CASSETTE, RECORDED
A permanently encased, recorded videotape which winds
from reel to reel, often automatically. Videotape cassettes must be played on a videoplayer compatible with
the particular type of cassette. Also called videocas-
sette.

VIDEOTAPE EDITOR
A videotape recorder with special features which allows
the electronic editing and recording of videotapes.

VIDEOTAPE RECORDED
A magnetic tape on which video and audio signals are
recorded for television use.

VIDEOTAPE RECORDER (VTR)
A device which can record images and sound on videotape and which can play back the videotape for viewing on a television monitor or special receiver. The videotape recorder may use reels or cartridges or cassettes. Most videotape recorders used in instructional programs are helical-scan type.

WEEDING
The selection of library material from the collection to be discarded or transferred to storage.

WITHDRAWAL
The process of removing from library records all entries for a resource no longer in the library.

WORK AREA
That portion of a library's total floor space allocated for use by library staff members for performance of their duties. It includes space for desks, furniture, and any needed equipment, as well as space for sorting and packing materials.

Z-39
A committee of the American National Standards Institute responsible for developing standards in the fields of library work, documentation, and related publishing practices.

CONTRIBUTORS

HELEN W. CYR is Head of the Audio-Visual Department at the Enoch Pratt Free Library in Baltimore, Maryland, which provides film services to the entire state of Maryland. She is a graduate of the University of California at Berkeley, where she also obtained her graduate degree in library science. Earlier she served as Director of Instructional Media for the Oakland Public Schools in California, for which she developed several nationally acclaimed multimedia projects and produced instructional film strips and innumerable bibliographies. She is also author of research studies and articles for professional journals in the field of librarianship. Mrs. Cyr is presently on the Executive Board of the Baltimore Film Forum, Inc., and the Baltimore International Film Festival.

PATRICIA DEL MAR, formerly Head of the Film Department, is now Head of Technical Services at the Long Beach Public Library, Long Beach, California. On the Board of Directors of EFLA, and active in the ISAD and RSTS divisions of ALA, she has been prominent in the A/V Chapter of the California Library Association.

WESLEY A. DOAK is presently the Audiovisual Consultant for the California State Library. Active in ALA, AECT and other professional associations, he has long been interested in the problem of comparability in media resources and services.

LEON L. DROLET, JR. is the Director of the Suburban Audio Visual Service [SAVS] which is owned and operated by the North Suburban Library System and the Suburban Library System of Illinois. A total of 170 public libraries are served by SAVS. He is the chairperson of the Audiovisual Committee of the Public Library Association, a division of the American Library Association. He also served as chairperson of the Illinois Library Association's Audiovisual Committee.

LAURA MURRAY is Coordinator of Audiovisual Services for
the Metropolitan Toronto Library Board.   She currently super-
vises AV technicians' services, the graphics unit, the Metro
equipment pool, the photography unit, a 16mm film/video collection for use by the six public library systems of Metro
Toronto, and the talking books service.

MYRA NADLER was the first reviewer for the Wilson Library
Bulletin film column.   She edited ALA's Guidelines for Audio-
visual Materials and Services for Large Public Libraries,
Recommendations for Audiovisual Materials and Services for
Small and Medium-Sized Public Libraries and CLA's Public
Library Subject Headings for 16mm Motion Pictures.   She
has contributed to the North American Film and Video Directory and written articles for New Media in Public Li-
braries, Educational Media Yearbook, Sightlines and the
California Librarian.
    She served as chairperson of the ALA PLA Audio Visual
Committee, on the Board of Directors of the Educational
Film Library Association and on the Film Library Information Council.   She was also president of the California Society of Librarians.
    She is currently working on an ALA basic list of Films
for Libraries.   Formerly the Supervisor of the Audio Visual
Department at the Palos Verdes Library District in California,
she is now Director of the Civic Center Library of the Torrance Public Library, Torrance, California.

MASHA RUDNITZKY PORTE has headed the film library of
the Dallas, Texas, Public Library since 1953.   A native of
Dallas, Ms. Porte formerly served as director of music and
art for a local adult education agency where she administered
an annual chamber music series presenting internationally
noted ensembles, a contemporary music series presenting
area artists and a young artist competition which evolved into
the Dallas Symphony Orchestra-sponsored G. B. Dealey
Awards.   She is also vice-president for public relations of
the Dallas Chamber Music Society.
    At the library, where her principal duties are collection
development and departmental administration, Ms. Porte presented an annual Focus on Film series which continued for
eighteen years.   Her total responsibility for this project included planning the programs, writing program notes, press
releases and mailing pieces, and introducing the showings.
    A founding member of the Film Library Information
Council, Ms. Porte served for eight years as editor of film
reviews to other publications.   Ms. Porte also acts as con-

sultant on special assignment to film distributors and to libraries.

WILLIAM SLOAN is in charge of the New York Public Library's Film Library, a unit he set up and has headed since 1958. He is also an adjunct professor at the Pratt Institute Graduate Library School and is the Editor of <u>Film Library Quarterly</u>.